HALOGEN
Cooking For Two

Also by Sarah Flower

THE EVERYDAY HALOGEN OVEN COOKBOOK
Over 200 quick and easy recipes for all the family
ISBN: 978-1-905862-47-4

PERFECT BAKING WITH YOUR HALOGEN OVEN
How to create tasty bread, cupcakes, bakes, biscuits and savouries
ISBN: 978-1-905862-55-9

THE EVERYDAY HALOGEN FAMILY COOKBOOK
Over 200 delicious and nutritious recipes
ISBN: 978-1-905862-70-2

EAT WELL, SPEND LESS
Over 250 healthy recipes for busy cooks who want to save money
ISBN: 978-1-905862-39-9

LIVE MORE, SPEND LESS
A savvy guide to saving money for all the family
ISBN: 978-1-905862-34-4

HALOGEN
Cooking For Two

SARAH FLOWER

SPRING HILL

Published by Spring Hill, an imprint of How To Books Ltd
Spring Hill House, Spring Hill Road
Begbroke, Oxford OX5 1RX
United Kingdom
Tel: (01865) 375794
Fax: (01865) 379162
info@howtobooks.co.uk
www.howtobooks.co.uk

First published 2011

How To Books greatly reduce the carbon footprint of their books
by sourcing their typesetting and printing in the UK.

British Library Cataloguing in Publication Data
A catalogue record of this book is available from the British Library.

ISBN: 978 1 905862 63 4

Produced for How To Books by Deer Park Productions, Tavistock, Devon
Designed and typeset by Mousemat Design Ltd
Printed and bound by in Great Britain by Bell & Bain Ltd, Glasgow

NOTE: The material contained in this book is set out in good faith for general
guidance and no liability can be accepted for loss or expense incurred as a result of
relying in particular circumstances on statements made in the book. Laws and
regulations are complex and liable to change, and readers should check the current
position with relevant authorities before making personal arrangements.

Contents

Introduction

The halogen has been promoted as a machine that cooks up to 40% quicker than conventional ovens, yet to me it is much more than that. It is incredibly energy-efficient. The halogen's large glass bowl offers me a complete view of anything I cook. The oven steams, grills, bakes, roasts, defrosts and even washes itself. And one thing it is absolutely perfect for is cooking for two.

Once you have mastered the basics, this machine will change the way you work in your kitchen. When cooking for two, you no longer have to waste energy heating a conventional oven. You can create amazing dishes with the minimum of fuss, washing up and waste.

Most of my recipes are quick and easy to prepare and I like to keep to a simple style of cookery that brings tasty results without you getting too frazzled.

Many of my readers have contacted me to ask how they could adapt some of the core recipes featured in *The Everyday Halogen Oven Cookbook* so that they could cook them for two people. I have carefully selected some of the most popular recipes from that book and reworked them to serve two. I have also included a large number of new and exciting recipes which work really well for two – these form the majority of the recipes in this book. If you can't find your favourite recipe from my first book in the following pages but would like it adapted to serve two people please let me know via my website www.sarahflower.co.uk.

Eat one, freeze one

I am a great believer in making life easier and saving money where you can. I am, too, a great fan of making use of the fridge or freezer and planning ahead. I would also strongly advise doubling up some recipes, enabling you to eat one and freeze one for another meal. You may also find some of my other halogen books useful – most recipes in these other books serve four but, with the eat one, freeze one principle, you can simply save time and create two meals in the time it takes to prepare one.

I hope you enjoy this journey and if this book has whetted your appetite for halogen cookery, why not have a look at my other books in this series including *The Everyday Halogen Oven Cookbook, Perfect Baking your Halogen Oven* and the latest, *The Everyday Family Halogen Cookbook.*

If you have any questions about using your halogen oven or about any of the recipes in this book, please contact me through my website: www.sarahflower.co.uk

Good luck.

Sarah

Using Your Halogen Oven

with As in my other halogen cookbooks, this first chapter shows newbie halogen oven users how to get the most from their machine. If you have bought another one of my books, you may want to skip this chapter as it contains duplicate information, or you might like to quickly scan it just to remind yourself of the joys of the halogen.

Choosing the right machine for you

There are many different halogen ovens on the market, but they are basically all the same machine. The two main variations are the bowl size and whether the lid is on a hinge. My first machine was from JML when they first started to become popular. I was not really sure what to expect and, over time, it has gained more and more use in our home. Personally I would opt for the largest bowl as this increases the oven's usability. You can also purchase extenders, which can help maximise use. Extenders are metal rings that fit over the top of the halogen bowl, literally extending the height of the bowl and enabling you to fit more into your oven. The lid then fits on top of the extender. They are also useful if you want to keep the food away from the heating elements to prevent burning.

After using the JML, I progressed to use the Flavorwave Turbo Platinum Oven. Some of the advantages of this particular oven are that it has a hinged lid, digital settings, three-speed fan and a preheat setting.

Looking at online forums I have noticed that the lids do seem to be a bit of a bugbear. I used a lid stand positioned beside my JML machine, though annoyingly these are optional extras that you have to purchase and are quite flimsy to look at. Personally, I think it is better to buy the halogen cooker with the hinged lid if you can afford it – this is definitely a safer and easier option. One particular reader, a gentleman in his eighties, phoned my publisher on using one of my other halogen cookbooks to find out where to buy a Flavorwave because he found the lid on his existing oven too heavy to keep lifting on and off. For that reason he wanted the hinged lid that the Flavorwave offers.

How do they work?

The halogen oven is basically a large glass bowl with an electric halogen

Using Your Halogen Oven • 9

lid. The lid is heavy as it contains the halogen element, timer and temperature settings. It can be fiddly to clean but I will come to that later. The halogen bulbs heat up the bowl and the fan moves the air around the bowl to create an even temperature. As it is smaller than a conventional oven, it heats up faster, reducing the need for long preheating and in some cases reducing the overall cooking time.

This makes it a very popular choice for those watching their pennies, living on their own or, like me, cooking for a busy family. It has even become a popular choice for students and caravanners. I read on a forum that some caravanners use the self-clean facility just like a mini dishwasher – ingenious! It is also popular as a second oven and really becomes invaluable at busy times like Christmas.

For safety, the lid's handle has to be securely fixed in place for the machine to switch on. This means that when you lift the lid, the oven is automatically switched off. If, however, you are using the Flavorwave machine with the hinged lid, you have to press the start button and remember to turn the machine off before you lift the lid.

The halogen does cook slightly differently to a conventional oven, so initial use often involves a process of trial and error, but it is not vastly different. If you have favourite recipes that you cook in the conventional oven, try them in the halogen. I find cooking at a slightly lower temperature or cooking for less time normally gives the same results, but hopefully this book will help give you more confidence.

The halogen oven is not a microwave and does not work in the same way as a microwave, so if you are thinking you can cook food in minutes you are wrong. It does however have a multitude of functions: defrosting, baking, grilling, roasting and steaming – the halogen is perfect for all these. Remember that to get the optimum benefit, air needs to circulate around the bowl, so ideally place dishes and trays on racks and avoid the temptation to overfill.

Getting the right equipment
This sounds obvious but ... make sure you have oven trays, baking sheets and casserole dishes that will fit inside your halogen oven. There are few

things more frustrating than planning a meal and just at the last minute realising that your dish does not fit in the machine! You can use any ovenproof dish or tray – metal, silicon and Pyrex are all fine. The halogen oven is round so it makes sense to look at trays and stands of the same shape, just smaller so you can remove them without burning yourself!

Out of everything, I think this is the halogen's biggest drawback. When I first started using one, it was frustrating to find that 80% of my bakeware did not fit in the machine, but a quick revamp and purchase of the accessories proved invaluable. If money is tight, you will often find great casserole dishes at car boot sales or charity shops – you don't have to spend a fortune on new cookware.

You can also buy an accessories pack, which contains steamer pans, grilling pans, toasting racks and even an extension ring. These are highly recommended if you use your oven regularly and certainly enhance what you can do with the machine. There are many websites selling or advertising these accessories, so a general internet search will point you in the right direction. Amazon is also a great place to look.

Let there be light

As experienced halogen users will know, the halogen light turns on and off during cooking. This is not a fault in the thermostat as some people have mentioned on forums. It simply turns off when the programmed temperature is reached, then on again when it drops. Set the temperature and marvel at how quickly the oven reaches the required temperature – literally in minutes. I love the light – as well as being able to watch your food cook, there is something quite cosy about walking into your kitchen on a winter or autumn evening and seeing the glow of the halogen cooker.

Timings

The halogen oven comes with a 60-minute timer and temperature setting dials. The Flavorwave Turbo also comes with three fan settings and a digital timer. All halogens turn off when the timer settings have been reached. This means that you can be reassured that if the phone rings or you are called away from the kitchen, your food won't spoil.

Size

The oven is small enough to sit on a worktop, but do allow space for removal of the lid if it is not hinged. The lid can get very hot and is quite large and heavy, being the brains of the machine, so it can be a good idea to buy the lid stand. However, be careful when using this stand as it can seem quite flimsy until you get used to it. You could opt to place the lid on a heatproof surface but, again, be careful not to burn yourself or your worktop!

Careful does it

Your oven should come with some tong-style gadget to help you lift out the racks. They are quite useful, but I also use a more substantial set of tongs. As with any oven or cooker, do be careful as the bowl and contents get very hot. I find using proper oven gloves a necessity as they cover your whole hand and wrist and can prevent accidents.

As with all electrical and hot appliances, do not let your children near the halogen – the glass bowl gets very hot.

Foil and coverings

Some people like to use foil when cooking. This can be a good idea as it prevents food from browning too quickly or it can be used to parcel food, but make sure the foil is secure. The fan is very strong and if the foil is not secure it could float around the oven and might damage the element. Another option for preventing burning is obviously to turn the temperature down or place the food further away from the element (by using the low rack or adding an extension ring).

Cleaning your oven

Your oven is promoted as being self-cleaning. This basically means that you fill it with a little water and a squirt of washing-up liquid and then turn it on to the wash setting. The combination of the fan and the heat allows the water to swish around the bowl, giving it a quick clean. This normally takes about 10 minutes. Personally I find it just as simple to remove the bowl and place it in the dishwasher or washing-up basin – it always comes out gleaming.

The lid is a little more difficult to clean and I would refer you to the manufacturer's guidelines as each product differs a little. Do not get the element or electrical parts wet!

High and low racks

There are two standard racks which come with every halogen oven – a high and a low rack. The high rack is placed nearer the element so use this if you want to brown something. The low rack is used more for longer cooking times.

You can cook directly on the bottom of the bowl. I do this quite often, particularly if I am being lazy and just want to chuck in some oven chips or if I am roasting something. It does cook well but takes a little longer compared to using the racks, as air is not able to circulate all around the food.

Baking

Some people worry about using the halogen to bake cakes but I think this is because they are setting the oven temperature too high, resulting in a crusty brown cake top with a soggy middle. Setting the oven to a lower temperature can solve this problem. Muffins and cupcakes take between 12 and 18 minutes. You only really encounter problems with cakes if you are cooking for too long at too high a temperature. Try some of my cake recipes and you will see how simple it can be.

To preheat or not to preheat

Most recipes I have found on forums don't mention preheating the oven. This is probably due to how quickly the oven reaches its temperature setting. However, I think it is worth turning the oven on a few minutes before use just to bring it up to the right temperature.

I found this to be the case when attempting to cook soft-boiled eggs. According to the Flavorwave recipe book, I should be able to cook a soft egg in 6 minutes just by placing it on the high rack. It didn't work, but when I tried again in a heated oven it was much more successful. As the halogen only takes a few minutes to reach the set temperature, I believe it is best to preheat and therefore most of my recipes advise this.

Some machines (such as the Flavorwave) have a preheat button which preheats at 260°C for 6 minutes, but others, such as the JML, require you to set the oven to the required temperature and then turn it on.

WEIGHT		LIQUID MEASURE	
Metric (approx.)	Imperial	Metric (approx.)	Imperial
25–30g	1oz	5ml	1 teaspoon (tsp)
50–55g	2oz	15ml	1 tablespoon (tbsp)
85g	3oz	25–30ml	1 fl oz
100g	3.5oz	50ml	2 fl oz
125g	4oz	75ml	3 fl oz
150g	5oz	100–125ml	4 fl oz
175g	6oz	150ml	5 fl oz
200g	7oz	175ml	6 fl oz
225g	8oz	200ml	7 fl oz
250g	9oz	225ml	8 fl oz
280g	10oz	250ml	9 fl oz
350g	12oz	300ml	10 fl oz (½ pint)
400g	14oz	600ml	20 fl oz (1 pint)
450g	16oz/1lb	1 litre	1¾ pints
900kg	2lb		

I hope this chapter has not confused you. Move on to try some recipes and then come back to this chapter at a later date – it will probably make more sense then!

Enjoy!

CHAPTER 2

Snacks

Halogen ovens aren't just for cooking main meals or desserts – they are perfect for quick and easy snacks. My *Everyday Halogen Oven Cookbook* offers quite a comprehensive range of snack recipes but here are some other varieties and suggestions, along with some reminders and simple tips you can adapt to suit. Unlike microwaves, halogen ovens can heat up pastries, pizzas and snacks without them resulting in a soggy mess. They can also make delicious toasties, warmed bagels, bruschetta and even boil an egg! Here are some reminders and some new ideas for you to try.

Toast

This is really where the accessories come into their own. If you purchase an accessory pack, a breakfast rack may come with it. This looks like a toast rack with some places for eggs. If you don't have this accessory, you could opt for an ovenproof toast rack and use it on the lower halogen rack – make sure there is at least a 2cm gap between it and the halogen lid. You may have to cut the slices of bread in half to accommodate them.

- Simply put your slices of bread on the rack.
- Cook at 220°C for 6–8 minutes, until your toast reaches the desired colour.

This is trial and error. When I first tried it, some of the slices were toasted but not golden – they still tasted the same but the odd slice lacked colour. I experimented with the temperature setting until things improved.

Toasted Sandwich

- If you want a toasted sandwich, place one slice with topping and one slice without topping side by side on the high rack.
- Cook at 200°C for 4–5 minutes until the toppings are bubbling.
- Place the plain bread slice over the topped slice to form a sandwich and cook for a further 1–2 minutes if necessary.

Tomato and Onion Welsh Rarebit

2–4 slices of bread
3–4 tablespoons milk
10g butter
100–150g mature
  cheese, grated
½ small onion, finely
  chopped (or a few
  spring onions)
1 tomato, chopped
1 teaspoon mustard
Black pepper to
  season

A new take on the Welsh rarebit – perfect for using up any leftovers!

- Preheat the halogen oven to 250°C.
- Place the bread on the high rack and cook for 2–3 minutes. Meanwhile, in a saucepan add the milk, butter, cheese, onion, tomato and mustard and stir until dissolved and thick. Season with black pepper. Be careful not to have the temperature too high or it will stick and burn.
- Take the bread out of the oven, turn it over and spoon on the cheese mixture. Season to taste. Place back on the high rack and cook for another 3 minutes until golden and bubbling.
- Serve with a side salad and some delicious chutney.

Bacon, Rocket and Tomato Deluxe

- Preheat the halogen oven to 230°C.
- Brush the bacon with a little olive oil and place on a grilling or browning tray on the highest rack. Cook until the bacon almost reaches your desired crispiness (5–8 minutes, turning over halfway through).
- Place the French bread or bagel alongside the bacon for a minute or two, as this will start to warm/toast one side of the bread.
- Remove when ready and plate up: turn the bread over and place the bacon on top, cover with the tomato slices and finish with the rocket. Season and, if you are a fan of olive oil, drizzle with some extra virgin olive oil. Serve immediately!

Extra virgin olive oil
2–4 rashers of bacon (depending on appetite!)
1–2 slices/portions of French bread or bagel
1–2 tomatoes, thickly sliced
Handful of rocket (or lettuce if you prefer)
Seasoning to taste

Sardines in Tomato Sauce on Toast

2–4 slices of
  wholemeal or
  granary bread
120g tin of sardines
  in tomato sauce
Spring onions,
  chopped (optional)
Dollop of sundried
  tomatoes
  (optional)

- Preheat the halogen oven to 230°C.
- Place the bread on the high rack and cook for 2–3 minutes. Meanwhile, remove the sardines from the tin and mash slightly (you can add some finely chopped spring onions and a dollop of sundried tomatoes if you like).
- Remove the bread from the oven, turn the slices over and place the sardines on top.
- Place back on the high rack and cook for 3–4 minutes until golden and bubbling.
- Serve with a side salad.

Bacon

Who can resist a bacon butty? You can cook your bacon without adding more fat in approximately 6–8 minutes using the halogen oven.

- Place the bacon on the high rack and set the temperature to 240°C.
- Cook for 5 minutes, then turn over and cook for another 5 minutes or until the bacon reaches your desired crispiness.

Soft-boiled Eggs

2–4 slices of bread
2–3 eggs
10g butter

You would not really think that the halogen oven could be used to boil an egg, but you will be surprised. You can place the egg directly onto the rack, or you could opt for the breakfast rack as an optional accessory.

- Preheat the halogen oven to 180°C.
- Place the eggs on the high rack or breakfast rack.
- Cook for 6 minutes to achieve a soft-boiled egg. Take care when removing the eggs from the oven as they will be very hot.

Note: This did not work when I first tried it. I discovered that you really have to preheat the oven and it is best if the eggs are at room temperature. If they have been stored in a cold fridge you may have to cook them for a minute or two more. You will soon find the timing to suit your preference.

Hard-boiled Eggs

- Preheat the halogen oven to 180°C.
- Place the eggs on the high rack or breakfast rack.
- Cook for 10 minutes to achieve a hard-boiled egg. Take care when removing the eggs from the oven as they will be very hot.

Tuna Melt Panini

1 small tin of tuna
Mayonnaise
Cheddar cheese,
    grated
Seasoning to taste
1–2 panini rolls

Create your own café-favourite snack in your halogen.

- In a bowl, mix the tuna, mayonnaise (enough to reach a creamy consistency) and Cheddar to taste. Season well.
- Preheat the halogen oven using the preheat setting or set the temperature to 240–250°C.
- Slice open the panini rolls and toast for 2–3 minutes. Fill with the tuna mixture. Close the panini.
- Place on the high rack and cook for 4–6 minutes until golden and the tuna and cheese mixture has started to melt.
- Serve with a side salad and tortilla chips.

Muffin Pizzas

These are so easy to make, it makes you wonder why we bother messing around with pizza dough. Kids love them if you get them to decorate the tops to resemble faces. Feel free to use whatever topping you prefer; this is a basic recipe using just cheese and tomato pasta sauce – the rest is up to you!

1–2 muffins, sliced in half, horizontally
2–4 spoonfuls of pasta sauce
Mature Cheddar, grated
Black pepper to season

- Place the muffins ready to assemble on a worktop or tray. Add a layer of the pasta sauce (my cheat's way!) followed by any other ingredients you require and finish with a generous handful of grated cheese. Season to taste.
- Place the muffins directly on the high rack (or on a browning tray if you prefer). Set the temperature to 230°C and cook until golden and bubbling (this should only take 5–7 minutes).
- Serve immediately.

Cheese, Sundried Tomatoes and Rocket Bagel

1–2 bagels
Cheddar cheese,
 grated or sliced
3–6 sundried
 tomatoes (drained
 of oil)
Rocket

This is my favourite bagel combination. Perfect with a lovely sesame or seeded bagel.

- Slice open the bagels and place inside upwards on the highest rack of your halogen. Set the oven to 240–250°C. Cook for 4–5 minutes until they start to brown.
- Remove and add the cheese, sundried tomatoes and rocket. Season to taste.
- Serve immediately while still warm!

Fresh Garlic Bread

You can make your own garlic bread by following this basic recipe.

French stick
1 tablespoon butter
1 or 2 crushed garlic
   cloves
Sprinkle of mixed
   herbs

- Partially slice a French stick into 2–3cm thick slices (making sure you don't cut right through to the base).
- Mix the butter with the garlic and a sprinkle of mixed herbs. Thickly spread this garlic butter in between the slices of bread.
- Place on a baking tray, first making sure it fits into your halogen oven.
- Place the tray on the medium rack and turn the halogen to 220°C. Cook for 5–8 minutes, until golden.
- To serve, simply allow the diners to tear the bread slices.

Variation: Try spreading with either green or red pesto instead of garlic butter.

Frozen Garlic Bread

- Place the bread, partially sliced, on a baking tray, first making sure it fits into your halogen oven.
- Place the tray on the medium rack and turn the oven on to 220°C. Cook for 5–8 minutes, until bread is golden. If baking the bread from frozen, add an extra 5–8 minutes.
- To serve, simply allow the diners to tear the bread slices.

Warming Naan Bread

Naan bread is delicious with curries and Indian meals. You can now buy ready-made naan bread and the halogen oven is a great tool for warming it.

- Sprinkle the naan bread with a little cold water.
- Place on the high rack and cook for 5–8 minutes at 220°C.
- Serve immediately.

Frozen Pizza

Refer to your oven manufacturer's instructions for more information.

- Place the pizza (frozen or defrosted) on the medium rack. If you have the halogen accessory pack, you could place it on the browning tray. If not, place it directly on the rack or use a pizza tray.
- You may want to place the upper rack, upside down, on top of the pizza for the first 10 minutes. This prevents the pizza toppings from lifting with the force of the fan – this is particularly advisable if your pizza has lots of loose toppings. The Flavorwave Turbo Platinum has three fan settings, so you could opt to choose the low fan setting which avoids needing to cover the top of the pizza.
- Set the temperature to 220°C and cook for 10–15 minutes, until golden.

Frozen Oven Chips

If you have children or teenagers in the house, there will come a time when they'll want you to cook some oven chips. The halogen oven cooks these in approximately 20 minutes.

- Turn the halogen oven to 220°C.
- Place the oven chips (frozen or defrosted) on a baking tray on the medium rack. Alternatively, you can place them on the bottom of the halogen oven if you prefer.
- I sprinkle the chips with a touch of paprika and a tiny dash of olive oil to add flavour and prevent the chips from becoming too dry.
- Cook for 20–25 minutes, turning occasionally if you feel like it, until they are golden.

Toasted Cheese and Ham Croissants

1–2 croissants
Mature cheese
2–3 slices of ham
Seasoning to taste

As with the panini, bruschetta and toasted sandwiches, this recipe is designed to show you what you can do with the halogen. Feel free to change the ingredients to suit your palate. Why not try a sweet filling? One of my children's favourites is chocolate spread with slices of banana.

- Preheat the halogen using the preheat setting or set the temperature to 250°C.
- Slice the croissants in half horizontally and fill them with cheese and ham.
- Place the filled croissants on the high rack and cook for 3–6 minutes until crispy and the cheese has started to melt.
- Serve immediately.

Crumpets

There is nothing like the taste of hot, buttered crumpets. You could add some crumbled stilton for a savoury variation – yummy!

- Preheat the halogen using the preheat setting or turn the temperature to the highest setting when you are ready to grill.
- Place the crumpets on the high rack and grill until they reach your preferred toasting.
- If you are adding a topping, do so after the crumpets have started to brown and not at the beginning of the process.
- Serve hot.

Baked Camembert

250g whole
   camembert cheese

I'm a bit embarrassed to call this a recipe, but once you have tasted it you will understand why it is a favourite.

- If your camembert comes in a wooden box, remove all packaging before placing the camembert back into the box. Alternatively, wrap the cheese in foil and place on a baking tray. I actually have a little ovenware pot that came with some camembert and which I reuse.
- There is no need to preheat the oven. Simply place the camembert, in foil or an ovenware pot, on the middle rack and bake for 10 minutes at 180°C.
- Serve with a selection of vegetable sticks, crusty bread or lightly steamed asparagus spears – or all three!

Meat

The halogen oven can cook meat slightly quicker than the conventional oven, though you have to be careful to get your temperature settings right. Too high and the tops of the joint or bird will burn, while the middle may remain raw or undercooked. I would advise using an oven thermometer to test your meat, particularly poultry or joints of meat until you are more confident.

When meat is placed on the lower rack, it allows the juices and fats to drain away – therefore making the meat healthier. I have found that meat does tend to be very tender and moist when cooked in the halogen oven – unless you overcook it!

If you are cooking a joint you can cook it as you would do in a conventional oven – roughly 20 minutes per 500g at 180°C and adding 10 minutes to the end of the cooking time.

As with all foods cooked in the halogen oven, make sure there is adequate space between the element and the food – ideally at least 2–3cm. The nearer the food is to the element, the more likely it is to burn or cook too quickly. If you are concerned, wrap some foil over the food for the first half of the cooking time, but do make sure the foil is secured well as the power of the fan could lift it.

Parma-wrapped Chilli Chicken

1–2 tablespoons quark or low fat cream cheese

½–1 red chilli, finely chopped

½ teaspoon chilli powder

Few drops of Tabasco sauce to taste (optional)

Seasoning to taste

2 chicken breasts

4 slices Parma ham

Olive oil

A very simple dish that takes minutes to prepare.

- Preheat the halogen oven using the preheat setting or set the temperature to 200°C.
- Place the quark or cream cheese in a bowl and mix in the chilli and Tabasco sauce until combined. Season to taste.
- Using a sharp knife, cut a slit in each chicken breast to form a pocket. Stuff the pockets with the creamed mixture.
- Wrap securely with Parma ham. Place seam-side down on a greased ovenproof dish. Drizzle with olive oil and season to taste.
- Place on the low rack and cook for 20–30 minutes until the chicken is cooked.

Balsamic Steaks

SERVES 2

This is a really simple dish – just remember to marinate either overnight or for at least 2 hours before cooking.

- In a bowl, mix the sugar, garlic, chilli powder, paprika, balsamic vinegar, olive oil and seasoning to form a paste.
- Dip the steaks into the mixture and leave coated overnight or for at least 2 hours before cooking.
- When ready to cook, heat the halogen to 250°C. Place the steaks on the highest rack and grill on both sides until done to your desired taste.
- Serve with a green salad.

1 tablespoon brown sugar
2–3 garlic cloves, crushed
1 teaspoon mild/medium chilli powder
1 teaspoon paprika
3 tablespoons balsamic vinegar
1 tablespoon olive oil
Seasoning to taste
2 lean steaks

Pan-roasted Vegetables and Chicken Breasts Wrapped in Parma Ham

200g new potatoes, washed and halved
1 red onion, deseeded and cut into wedges
1 red pepper, cut into wedges
8–12 cherry tomatoes
3–4 cloves of garlic, left whole
Olive oil
2–3 sprigs of thyme
2 chicken breasts
2–4 slices of Parma ham
Paprika
Seasoning to taste

A simple one-pot dish.

- Place the vegetables and garlic cloves in an oiled ovenproof dish or roasting tin, first making sure it fits well in your halogen oven. Drizzle with oil and add the sprigs of thyme. Toss well to ensure everything is evenly coated.
- Place on the middle rack. Set the temperature to 220°C and cook for 10 minutes.
- Meanwhile, sprinkle the chicken breasts with paprika and wrap in the Parma ham. Season to taste.
- Remove the halogen's lid and make a gap in the vegetables for the chicken. Carefully place (don't burn yourself) the wrapped chicken breasts, seam-side down, among the vegetables. Drizzle with olive oil.
- Replace the lid and cook at 200°C for 20–30 minutes, or until the chicken is cooked to your liking. If the vegetables start to brown too much, you can cover the dish with foil, but the tomatoes and peppers become very sweet when they start to darken which adds to the flavour.
- Serve when the chicken is cooked to your satisfaction.

Garlic and Rosemary Chicken Parcels

A simple dish with great flavours that can be prepared in advance.

- Measure and cut some foil double the size of each chicken breast. The foil also needs to be double thickness.
- Brush the centre of each piece of foil with olive oil.
- Place 1–2 slices of red onion on top of the olive oil. Place the chicken breasts on top of the onion. Season with the chicken seasoning.
- In a small bowl or cup, mix the butter with the garlic. Place a spoonful of this butter mixture onto each of the chicken fillets.
- Sprinkle with the chopped rosemary and season to taste.
- Pull the sides of the foil up to form a bowl shape, before adding the wine or vermouth. Then scrunch the foil securely closed and place on a baking tray. You can either leave the chicken to marinate until you are ready to cook, or cook it immediately.
- Place on the middle rack and set the halogen to 220°C. Cook for 10 minutes.
- Remove the halogen's lid and very carefully unwrap the foil, exposing the chicken but leaving the foil edges high to avoid the juices leaking. Cook for another 10–15 minutes or until the chicken is cooked to your liking.
- Serve with sautéed potatoes and steamed seasonal vegetables.

SERVES 2

Olive oil
2–4 slices of red onion
2 chicken breasts
Chicken seasoning (I use Schwartz No Added Salt Chicken seasoning)
10g butter
3–4 cloves of garlic, crushed
1 teaspoon freshly-chopped rosemary
Seasoning to taste
4 tablespoons white wine or vermouth

Beef and Ale Casserole

350g shin of beef or stewing steak, diced
1 tablespoon plain flour
½ teaspoon paprika
Seasoning to taste
2 tablespoons olive oil
1 small onion, finely chopped
2 small to medium-sized carrots, diced
1 stick of celery, diced
175ml real ale or stout
1 tablespoon tomato purée
2 teaspoons brown sugar
300ml beef stock
Bouquet garni (thyme, parsley, bay leaf)
100g mushrooms, chopped
10g butter

This is a traditional casserole that benefits from a slow cook. You can cook this on the hob if you prefer but the halogen works well. If your halogen has a digital timer you can, of course, set it to suit your timing, but if it has a dial timer (which is more common) you will have to reset this after 60 minutes.

- If your meat is not already diced, cut it into chunks and remove any excess fat.
- Place the flour, paprika and seasoning in a bowl or freezer bag. Add the meat, shake and coat until it is covered well.
- Heat the oil in a sauté pan on the hob and brown the meat on all sides. Then place the meat into a casserole dish. (Make sure that your casserole dish fits in the halogen. Ideally choose one with a lid for later use, but if your dish does not have a lid you could instead use an extension ring or a double layer of foil, securely folded.)
- Using the same pan as you browned the meat in, add the onion, carrots and celery and cook for about 5 minutes on a medium/high heat before adding the ale, tomato purée and sugar. Stir well, making sure you also scrape up any meat juices or leftovers as you go. Once heated, add this to the meat and top up with the beef stock. Combine well.

- Add *bouquet garni* and salt and pepper to the casserole. Cover the dish with a lid (or double layer of tin foil held securely) and place on the low rack. Turn the halogen to 160°C and cook for 1 hour.
- After the hour, fry the mushrooms in butter on the hob until tender and add to the casserole.
- Turn the heat up to 190°C and continue to cook for another 15 minutes.
- Serve with fluffy mashed potatoes and seasonal vegetables.

Creamy Chicken Casserole

Olive oil
2 chicken thighs,
    depending on
    appetite!
1 small onion, peeled
    and roughly
    chopped
1 garlic clove,
    crushed
1 leek, finely
    chopped
75ml white wine
250ml chicken stock
Seasoning
1 bay leaf
75g frozen peas
50ml double cream
Small handful of
    finely chopped
    tarragon
1 teaspoon cornflour
    (optional)

- Brown the chicken thighs to a nice golden colour. To do this there are two options: hob or halogen.
  * Hob: Simply add olive oil to the pan and, on a medium/high heat, cook the chicken on both sides until golden. Remove and place in your casserole dish (make sure it fits in your halogen!), along with the onion, garlic and leeks.
  * Halogen: Place the chicken in a pan on the high rack and brush with oil. Add the onion, garlic and leeks to the pan as you can soften them at the same time. Set the temperature to 230°C and cook the chicken on both sides until golden. Remove from the oven and place the chicken and vegetables into your casserole dish (making sure it fits into your halogen).
- Pour the wine and chicken stock over the chicken thighs. Season and add the bay leaf.
- Cover the casserole dish with a lid (or if your dish does not have a lid use an extension ring or a double layer of foil, held securely) and cook in the halogen at 160°C for 1 hour.
- When the hour is up, add the frozen peas, cream and tarragon. Combine well. If, at this stage your sauce is too thin, you could mix a teaspoon of cornflour with a little water and combine it into your casserole. It will thicken as it cooks. Cook for another 15 minutes.
- Serve with new potatoes and seasonal vegetables.

Chicken Breast stuffed with Cream Cheese and Mustard Sauce

- Wash the chicken breasts before cutting almost in half horizontally. Place on a sheet of greaseproof paper or clingfilm. With a rolling pin or meat mallet, flatten until thin.
- Mix the cream cheese with the mustard and chives and season to taste. Spread this mixture over the open chicken breasts.
- Carefully roll each breast up like a Swiss roll and secure with a wooden (previously soaked) cocktail stick. Place on a greased browning tray.
- Set the halogen oven to 200°C and place the tray on the middle rack. Cook for 15–20 minutes until breasts are golden.
- Serve with new potatoes and seasonal vegetables.

2 chicken breasts
1 tablespoon olive oil
3 tablespoons cream cheese
1 tablespoon Dijon mustard
2 teaspoons chopped chives
Sea salt
Black pepper

Spicy Meatballs with Rich Tomato Sauce and Spaghetti

SERVES 2

225g lean beef or lamb mince

2 cloves of garlic, chopped

½ chilli, finely chopped

½ teaspoon ground cumin

Zest of ½ lemon

Sea salt

Black pepper

200g cherry tomatoes

2–3 cloves of garlic, finely chopped

1 small red onion, finely chopped

½ red pepper, de-seeded and chopped

Olive oil

Balsamic vinegar

1 teaspoon sugar

1 teaspoon dried or small handful of freshly chopped oregano

100–150g spaghetti, depending on appetite

Grated parmesan to garnish

This meal can be cooked in advance. The two stages – the meatballs and the rich sauce – can both be prepared in advance and reheated when needed. If you are opting to do this, follow stages one and two and refrigerate until ready to cook. You can also freeze the meatballs. The sauce is best kept in a sealed container in your fridge for no more than three days.

- Place the mince into a large bowl and add 2 cloves of chopped garlic, chilli, cumin and lemon zest. Season to taste with sea salt and black pepper. Mix well and shape into balls. Leave these in the fridge for 10 minutes or until needed. (You can also freeze them on a baking sheet at this stage. Once frozen they can be transferred into a freezer bag, which prevents them from sticking to each other when frozen.)
- Meanwhile, make the rich tomato sauce. Place the tomatoes, 2–3 cloves of finely chopped garlic, red onion and red pepper in an ovenproof dish. Drizzle with olive oil and a dash of balsamic vinegar. Sprinkle with sea salt, sugar and some dried or fresh oregano. Place on the medium rack at 200°C and cook for 15 minutes (or 30 if you are preparing the sauce for later use).

- When you are ready to cook the meatballs, transfer them to a greased baking dish or browning tray. (First defrost the meatballs if they are frozen.) Place on the high rack and set the temperature to 230°C. Place the tomato mixture on the low rack so it can continue to cook or reheat if it has been prepared in advance. Bake until the meatballs are browned and cooked, turning occasionally. This should take no more than 15 minutes.
- While this is cooking, prepare the spaghetti as per the manufacturer's instructions.
- To serve, place the meatballs on a bed of spaghetti and pour over the tomato sauce. Garnish with a sprinkle of freshly grated parmesan.

Fruity Chicken

Olive oil
2 chicken breasts
Dash of paprika
1 small red onion,
   chopped
2–3 rashers of thick
   smoked bacon or
   lardons, thickly
   diced
4 no-soak prunes,
   chopped roughly
4 no-soak apricots,
   chopped roughly
1 teaspoon freshly
   chopped rosemary
150ml chicken stock
100ml white wine
Sea salt
Black pepper

- In a deep ovenproof dish, add the olive oil and chicken breasts. Sprinkle the chicken with a dash of paprika. Place on the highest rack you can fit the dish onto (this may be the medium rack depending on the height of your dish). Set the temperature to 210°C and brown the chicken on both sides.
- Once browned, add the onion and bacon and continue to cook for another 5–8 minutes until the onion and bacon start to soften.
- Add the remaining ingredients and season with sea salt and black pepper. Cover with a lid or a double layer of tin foil (firmly secured) and turn the temperature down to 180°C. Cook for 20–25 minutes.
- Serve with fluffy mashed potato and seasonal vegetables.

Red Pesto Chicken Parcels

- Cut out 2 double-thickness squares of foil, twice the size of each chicken breast. Grease each double-thickness square with a little butter.
- Place one chicken breast in the middle of each square. Add 1–2 teaspoons of red pesto to each chicken breast. Cover with some onion slices.
- Drizzle with a tablespoon of white wine. Season well and secure into a parcel.
- Preheat the halogen oven using the preheat setting or turn on to 200°C. Place the chicken parcels on the medium rack and cook for 20–25 minutes until cooked.

2 chicken breasts
Butter
2–4 teaspoons red pesto
1 small red onion, sliced
2 tablespoons white wine
Seasoning

Beefy Stuffed Onions with Goat's Cheese Topping

2 large onions,
    peeled
Knob of butter
Olive oil
175g lean minced
    beef
2 tomatoes, finely
    chopped
1 tablespoon tomato
    purée
50ml red wine
    (optional)
2 cloves of garlic,
    crushed
1–2 sprigs of thyme
1 teaspoon freshly
    chopped rosemary
Sea salt
Black pepper
100g goat's cheese

This is a lovely dish that is also very filling. If you are vegetarian you can opt to use veggie or Quorn mince instead of beef. This dish can be prepared in advance and reheated.

- Boil the onions in a pan of water for 5 minutes. Drain and leave until they are cool enough to handle.
- Cut off the top of each onion and remove the inside leaving a thick outer shell. Chop the discarded onion and leave to one side as you will need this later.
- Spread some butter inside the onions and place into a greased ovenproof dish.
- Heat a little olive oil in a sauté pan and cook the chopped onion until it softens. Add the mince and continue to cook until it has browned.
- Once browned, add the chopped tomatoes, tomato purée, red wine (optional), garlic, thyme, rosemary and seasoning. Cook for another couple of minutes until thoroughly combined and heated through.
- Spoon the mixture into the onion shells. Finish with a thick layer of goat's cheese, followed by a sprinkle of black pepper.
- Place on the medium rack at 190°C and bake for 20–25 minutes until the onion is soft and the goat's cheese is golden and bubbling.
- Serve with a green salad.

Chicken with Mustard Sauce

- Place the chicken breasts in an oiled ovenproof dish. Place this on the medium rack and cook at 210°C, turning the chicken until it is golden on both sides.
- Meanwhile, melt the butter in a pan. Add the flour and make a paste. Add the stock, gently whisking all the time. The sauce should be thick and shiny.
- Remove from the heat and add the mustard, cream and seasoning. Pour the sauce over the browned chicken.
- Turn the temperature down to 180°C and cook for another 15 minutes or until the chicken is cooked through to your satisfaction.
- Serve with sauté potatoes and seasonal vegetables.

Olive oil
2 chicken breasts
1 heaped dessert-
    spoon butter
1 dessertspoon
    cornflour
250ml hot chicken
    stock
2–3 heaped
    teaspoons
    wholegrain mustard
    (depending on
    your taste)
150ml double cream
Seasoning

Feta, Pancetta and Onion Puff

SERVES 2

50g fresh
   breadcrumbs
275ml milk
1 small onion, halved
   or quartered
1 bay leaf
1 teaspoon
   wholegrain mustard
2 eggs, separated
75g pancetta,
   chopped
50g feta cheese,
   crumbled
½ teaspoon dried
   thyme or small
   handful of freshly
   chopped thyme
Seasoning to taste

This is a light dish with a consistency similar to soufflés. It makes a nice one-pot, supper-time dish.

- Place the breadcrumbs in a bowl. Place the milk, onion and bay leaf in a pan and bring to the boil.
- Remove the onion (leaving it to one side) and bay leaf and stir in the mustard. Pour this over the breadcrumbs and leave to stand for 20–30 minutes.
- Separate the eggs. Mix the egg yolks and all other ingredients (leaving the egg whites to one side) together with the soaked breadcrumbs.
- Chop the remaining onion finely and add to the mixture.
- Beat the egg whites until light and fluffy. Fold into the mixture carefully.
- Pour this into a well-greased ovenproof dish.
- Preheat the halogen oven using the preheat setting or set the temperature to 200°C. Bake on the medium rack for 20–25 minutes.
- Serve with a green salad.

Pesto Pork

Perfect for the halogen oven – quick, simple and tastes great. Serve with a selection of roasted vegetables.

- Preheat the halogen oven using the preheat setting or set the temperature to 230°C.
- Place the chops or steaks on the grill tray. Grill on the high rack for 3–4 minutes each side until they are almost cooked. Remove and put to one side.
- Mix the cream cheese and the pesto together thoroughly.
- In another bowl, mix the breadcrumbs and parmesan together and season to taste.
- Pour the pesto mix onto the pork, ensuring the tops are covered. Sprinkle on the breadcrumb mixture to finish.
- Place back in the halogen on the high rack and cook until the topping is golden and bubbling. This should take no more than 5 minutes.

2 pork chops or loin steaks
½ small tub of cream cheese
2–3 teaspoons pesto
50g wholemeal breadcrumbs
25g parmesan cheese, grated
Seasoning to taste

Spring Chicken Casserole

2 chicken breasts
½ teaspoon paprika
Sea salt
Black pepper
Olive oil
150g new potatoes,
  finely sliced
1 small carrot, finely
  diced
½ bunch of spring
  onions, chopped
150ml white wine or
  vermouth
250–350ml chicken
  stock, warmed
Small handful of
  fresh tarragon
50g French beans
½ small head of
  broccoli, cut into
  small florets
50g peas
2–3 tablespoons
  crème fraîche

This is the perfect dish to use up any of the lovely spring vegetables. Sometimes spring can still be a bit chilly so there is nothing better than a delicious, warming evening meal. This recipe is perfect.

- Rub the chicken breasts with paprika. Season to taste. Place them in an oiled ovenproof dish and finish with an extra drizzle of oil.
- Add the sliced potatoes, carrot and spring onions.
- Place on the medium rack and set the temperature to 210°C. Cook for 15 minutes.
- Meanwhile, prepare the other ingredients. Once the 15 minutes are up, add the remaining ingredients apart from the crème fraîche. Combine well.
- Cover with a lid or double layer of foil and cook at 190°C for another 30 minutes.
- Remove from the oven and stir in the crème fraîche.
- Serve with crusty bread and salad.

Moussaka

- Place the aubergine slices in a pan of boiling water for 2 minutes. Remove and pat dry. Leave to one side.
- Meanwhile, heat a little olive oil in a sauté pan and fry the onion and garlic. Add the lamb mince and cook until brown.
- Add the tomatoes, tomato purée, mint, cinnamon and seasoning and cook for another 2–3 minutes.
- Select your ovenproof dish – I normally use a Pyrex or small lasagne dish for this. Make sure it fits into your halogen oven. Preheat the halogen using the preheat setting or set to 210°C.
- Place a layer of mince in the dish, followed by a layer of aubergine. Continue alternating mince and aubergine, finishing with a layer of mince.
- Mix the crème fraîche with the grated cheese and pour over the final layer of mince. Garnish with a sprinkle of parmesan.
- Place on the low rack and cook for 20–25 minutes until bubbling.

1 aubergine, sliced
Olive oil
1 small onion, finely chopped
1 clove garlic, crushed
200g lamb mince
½ tin chopped tomatoes
1 teaspoons tomato purée
1 teaspoon dried mint
1 teaspoon ground cinnamon
Seasoning to taste
150ml low fat crème fraîche
30g mature Cheddar or parmesan cheese, grated

Italian Chicken One Pot

Olive oil
2 chicken breasts
Paprika
1 small red onion, thickly sliced or cut into wedges
2–3 cloves of garlic, halved
1 pepper, cut into thick wedges
4 sundried tomatoes (in oil), halved
50g thick pancetta, diced
6–8 ripe vine tomatoes, whole
6–8 new potatoes, sliced
2 sprigs of thyme
Sea salt
Black pepper

A very simple dish. Why not prepare this in advance and leave it covered in the fridge until you are ready to cook – perfect for a lovely meal after a day at work.

- Drizzle olive oil into a roasting tin or ovenproof dish. Score the chicken breasts with a sharp knife. Rub with a little olive oil and sprinkle with paprika. Place the chicken in the roasting dish.
- Add the remaining ingredients, ensuring they are evenly distributed in the dish. Finish with a drizzle of olive oil and season with sea salt and black pepper.
- Place on the medium rack and set the temperature to 210°C. Cook for 20–30 minutes or until the chicken is cooked to your liking. Serve immediately.

Mediterranean-style Tortilla

This is an ideal dish for using up any leftover vegetables – anything goes, so experiment!

- Preheat your halogen oven using your preheat setting or set the temperature to 200°C.
- In a large bowl, add the eggs and beat well. Add the remaining ingredients and combine. Pour into a well-greased ovenproof dish.
- Place on the medium rack and cook for 20–25 minutes until firm.
- Serve hot or cold with salad.

2–3 eggs, beaten
½ bunch of spring onions, finely chopped
½ red pepper, diced or thinly sliced
3 rashers pancetta, diced
2–3 sundried tomatoes, chopped
25g parmesan, grated
Small handful of fresh herbs (basil, oregano or thyme would suit)
Seasoning to taste

Lamb Biryani

Olive oil
350g lamb, cubed
1 small onion, diced
1 clove of garlic,
  crushed
½ teaspoon ground
  cinnamon
½ teaspoon ground
  cardamom
½ teaspoon ground
  cloves
½ teaspoon curry
  powder
125ml plain Greek
  yoghurt
2 tomatoes, diced
120g long grain rice
Toasted almonds to
  sprinkle

- In a sauté pan, add the oil and heat until hot. Add the lamb, onion and garlic and cook until the lamb starts to brown and the onion starts to soften.
- Add the spices and cook for a couple of minutes before adding the yoghurt and tomatoes. Combine well and gently cook on a low heat.
- Meanwhile cook the rice following the manufacturer's instructions. (I normally add 1¼ water to rice, bring to the boil and leave simmering for a couple of minutes before popping a lid on and removing completely from the heat. Leave to stand for 10–12 minutes. Fluff up using a fork.)
- When the rice is done, place a layer in the bottom of your ovenproof dish. Follow this with a layer of the lamb mixture. Continue until you have used up all the ingredients.
- Cover with foil and place on the medium rack. Turn the temperature to 180°C and cook for 20 minutes.
- Garnish with the toasted almonds before serving.

Chicken, Mushroom and Bacon Lasagne

As with all lasagne cooked in the halogen, you can speed up the cooking process by using fresh lasagne sheets or parboiling packet ones before adding to the dish.

- Place the olive oil into a sauté pan and cook the mushrooms and bacon for 5–8 minutes. Remove from the heat.
- Melt the butter in a heavy-based saucepan. Add the flour and stir well with a wooden spoon. Gradually add the milk and bring slowly to the boil, stirring all the time. You may want to add more milk if you think the sauce is becoming too thick.
- Add the chicken, mushrooms and bacon to the sauce. Stir well before seasoning with black pepper and sea salt.
- In another bowl, combine the tomatoes, herbs and seasoning.
- Start to layer your lasagne by placing some of the tomato mixture in the base, followed by lasagne sheets, followed by the chicken mixture. Continue, finishing with lasagne sheets on the top.
- Mix the yoghurt and the egg and spread over the top. Sprinkle with parmesan and season with black pepper.
- Place the lasagne on the medium rack. Turn the temperature to 200°C and cook for about 40 minutes (less if you have parboiled the lasagne sheets or used fresh). If it starts to darken on top, cover securely with tin foil.
- Serve with potato wedges and green salad.

Olive oil
125g mushrooms, sliced (a mixture of different types is good)
4 rashers lean bacon, diced
Knob of butter
1 tablespoon plain flour or cornflour
200ml milk
125g cooked chicken, chopped
Black pepper
Sea salt
200g tinned tomatoes, drained and chopped
½ teaspoon dried mixed herbs
Lasagne sheets
125ml Greek yoghurt
1 small egg, beaten
1 level tablespoon grated parmesan cheese

Note: Ideal for using up any cooked chicken.

Garlicky Chicken

½ bulb of garlic,
  cloves peeled
150ml olive oil
Juice and zest of 1
  lemon
2 tablespoons crème
  fraîche
½ teaspoon mustard
Black pepper
Sea salt
2–4 chicken breasts
  (depending on
  appetite!)

This really is garlicky, so if you don't like garlic avoid this dish. You can use whatever chicken pieces you prefer. I like chicken breasts but that is just personal preference. Prepare this dish up to a day in advance to allow the flavours to really develop.

- Using a food processor or electric mini chopping gadget, combine the garlic, olive oil, lemon juice and zest and whizz until it forms a smooth creamy paste. Add the crème fraîche and mustard before seasoning with black pepper and sea salt.
- Wash the chicken pieces and place them in a greased ovenproof dish, just big enough to hold the chicken. Pour over the sauce, ensuring the chicken is well coated. Cover with a double layer of tin foil and place in the fridge to marinate.
- Remove from the fridge in time for the chicken to be at room temperature when you are ready to cook.
- Once ready, simply place the dish (with foil still intact) on the medium rack and cook at 200°C for 30–40 minutes until the chicken is tender and cooked to your requirements.
- Serve with green vegetables and mini roast potatoes.

Tender Chilli Chicken in Breadcrumbs

This is a really lovely dish, made all the better by marinating for at least an hour, or overnight, before adding the breadcrumbs. (Remember to stock your freezer with breadcrumbs made from any stale bread you have lurking in your bread bin. Bag them in freezer bags ready for toppings, coatings or even an indulgent treacle tart!)

- Flatten the chicken breasts using a rolling pin or wooden kitchen mallet. You need to get them as thin as possible.
- Place the olive oil, white wine or vermouth, garlic, chilli, lemon juice and seasoning in your food processor and whizz until smooth. Pour over the chicken, cover with foil or clingfilm and place in the fridge for at least an hour to marinate.
- Remove the chicken from the fridge so that it reaches room temperature before cooking. Meanwhile, place the remaining ingredients in a bowl and combine well. Sprinkle the breadcrumb mix over the chicken pieces, pressing down well where you can.
- Place the chicken on the medium rack and set the temperature to 200°C. Cook for 15–20 minutes.
- Serve with a crisp green salad and, for an extra chilli hit, some sweet chilli sauce.

SERVES 2

2 chicken breasts
1 tablespoon olive oil
1–2 tablespoons white wine or vermouth
2 cloves garlic, peeled
½ red chilli
Juice of ½ lemon
Sea salt
Black pepper
60g fresh breadcrumbs
Pinch dried thyme
Pinch cayenne pepper
20g grated parmesan

Spicy Polenta Chicken

1–2 teaspoons
coriander seeds
1 red chilli, finely
chopped
2 cloves garlic, finely
chopped
½–1 teaspoon sweet
curry powder
400g ready-to-use
polenta
1 small red onion,
cut into wedges
6–8 cherry tomatoes,
whole
Small handful of
coriander leaves
2 boneless chicken
breasts
2 tablespoons natural
Greek yoghurt
Black pepper
Sea salt
Olive oil

I had never cooked with polenta until I found a recipe using Italian flavours. Polenta can be a bit tasteless so I would advise, if you like your food to be tasty, seasoning well and using some spices. I love the flavour of coriander seeds and polenta, just like sweet potato, really works well with it.

- Using a pestle and mortar, grind the coriander seeds. Add half the chopped chilli, the garlic and sweet curry powder and combine well.
- In a roasting dish or deep baking tray, crumble the polenta into bite-sized chunks. Spread this evenly around the base of the dish. Sprinkle the spice mixture evenly over the polenta. Finish by interspersing the onion, tomatoes and a few coriander leaves among the polenta.
- Use a sharp knife to gently score the top of each chicken breast – 3 or 4 lines will be perfect. Place the chicken in the dish with the polenta. Carefully place the Greek yoghurt over the top of the chicken to form a coating.
- Season the whole dish with black pepper and sea salt and finish with a generous drizzle of olive oil.
- Place the dish on the medium rack and set the temperature to 220°C. Cook for 20–30 minutes until the chicken is golden.
- Serve immediately.

Pan-roasted Breakfast

Don't think this is only suitable for breakfast – it is ideal for a lovely supper, especially when you require comfort food.

- Place the tomatoes, garlic and bacon in an ovenproof dish (first making sure it fits in your halogen). Sprinkle with olive oil, sea salt and black pepper.
- Place on the medium rack at 200°C for 10–12 minutes.
- Remove from the oven. Make two spaces evenly in the mixture and crack an egg into each space.
- Cover the dish with foil or a lid and bake for a further 10–15 minutes until the eggs are cooked to your taste.
- Remove from the oven, garnish with chopped parsley and serve immediately with warm crusty bread.

1 punnet of cherry tomatoes
1–2 cloves garlic
½ pack of thick bacon, roughly chopped
Olive oil
Sea salt
Black pepper
2 large eggs
1 tablespoon chopped parsley

Lemon and Ginger Pork Chops

SERVES 2

30ml olive oil
½ bunch of spring
  onions, chopped
Juice and rind of 1
  lemon
2cm knuckle of fresh
  ginger, finely
  chopped
1 clove of garlic,
  crushed
Small handful of
  fresh coriander,
  finely chopped
100ml Greek yoghurt
  (I use Total as it
  holds during
  cooking)
Seasoning to taste
2 pork chops
Extra coriander
  leaves to garnish

You will need to marinate these, ideally for around 3–4 hours to get a lovely moist and flavoursome chop. Once marinated, simply pop in the oven and cook for 20 minutes – so easy!

• Mix all the ingredients together apart from the chops. Add the chops ensuring they are fully covered. (You can either do this in the bowl you made the marinade in, or place the marinade in a freezer bag, add the chops and shake well to cover.) Place the marinating chops in the fridge for at least 4 hours.
• Once ready to cook, place the chops in the base of an oiled ovenproof dish. Pour over the remaining marinade.
• Preheat the halogen oven to 190°C.
• Place on the medium rack and cook for 20 minutes, or until the chops are cooked to your desired taste.
• Serve with a garnish of coriander leaves.

One-pot Italian Lamb Steaks

This is a really easy dish. You can prepare it in advance and leave in the fridge to marinate, or simply throw it together 30 minutes before you want to eat.

- In an ovenproof dish, add all the ingredients apart from the lamb, and combine until evenly coated and distributed. Place the lamb in among the vegetables and press down until it is covered slightly with the juice. Place in the fridge, covered, until needed.
- When you are ready to cook, preheat the halogen to 210°C.
- Place the dish on the medium rack and cook for 20–30 minutes until the lamb is cooked to your satisfaction.
- Serve immediately with crusty bread and a green salad.

½ tin of tomatoes
100ml red wine
50g cherry tomatoes
1 small red onion, cut into thick slices or wedges
½ red pepper, cut into thick slices
1–3 cloves of garlic, whole
50g black olives, halved
2–3 sprigs of thyme
Sea salt
Black pepper
2 lamb steaks

Sweet & Chilli Chops

2 pork chops
Olive oil
1 red onion, finely
    chopped
½ teaspoon chilli
    flakes (more if you
    want a very hot
    sauce!)
80–100g golden
    syrup
Seasoning to taste

A friend passed this recipe on to me, I hope you enjoy its taste and simplicity!

- Place the chops in the base of an oiled ovenproof dish. Preheat the halogen oven to 190°C.
- Place on the medium rack and cook for 10–12 minutes, or until the chops are almost cooked to your desired taste.
- While they are cooking, fry your onion in a dash of olive oil. Add the chilli flakes. Remove from the heat and add the golden syrup. This will melt in the pan and become more fluid.
- When the chops are ready, pour the sauce over them. Place back in the halogen for another 5 minutes.
- Serve immediately.

Toad in the Hole

A family favourite that never fails to impress.

- Preheat your halogen oven to 190°C
- Place a drizzle of olive oil in your ovenproof dish and brush it around all the edges.
- Place the sausages in the dish and pop it on the middle rack. Cook for 10–15 minutes until the sausages start to brown and crisp.
- Meanwhile, mix the flour, eggs and milk. Season well and leave to one side.
- When the sausages are brown, remove from the oven and immediately pour the batter into the dish. This may sizzle a bit so be careful.
- Return this to the oven and cook for another 15–20 minutes until golden and firm to touch.
- Serve with mash, seasonal vegetables and gravy.

Olive oil
2–4 sausages, ideally lean
100g plain flour
2 eggs
180ml milk
Black pepper
Sea salt

Gammon Steaks with Parsley Sauce and Mini Roasts

400g new potatoes,
  washed
Olive oil

*Garlic & Herb
seasoning*
Paprika
20g butter
20g plain flour or
  cornflour
300ml milk
Small handful freshly
  chopped parsley
Black pepper
Sea salt
2 Gammon Steaks
Vegetables of your
  choice, if desired

- Place the potatoes on an oiled baking tray. Drizzle with olive oil and season with *Garlic & Herb seasoning*. Finish with a sprinkle of paprika. Shake the tray to ensure the potatoes are evenly covered. Add more olive oil if you think they are too dry.
- Set the temperature to 200°C. Place the potatoes on the medium rack and cook for 30-40 minutes, until the potatoes are cooked and golden.
- While the potatoes are roasting, make the sauce by melting the butter in a saucepan. Add the flour and using a wooden spoon stir well to form a paste.
- Gradually add the milk and continue to stir over a medium heat. If you start to get lumps, swap the wooden spoon for a balloon whisk and whisk well. Continue to stir/whisk until the sauce starts to thicken.
- Add the parsley and season to taste. Remove from heat.
- Set the temperature of the halogen to 230°C. Move the potatoes to the low rack and place the gammon steaks on the high rack as you are effectively going to grill them.

- Brush the steaks lightly with olive oil. Cook for approximately 4–5 minutes each side until they are cooked to your requirements. Timing depends on size and thickness of steaks.
- While they are cooking, gently reheat the sauce but do not allow to boil or it may catch and burn – I would suggest a low heat. If you are cooking vegetables to accompany the meal, you will need to have these ready.
- Remove the potatoes and steaks from the oven and place on your dinner plates. Pour the sauce over the steaks. Serve with peas or green vegetables.

Chicken, Leek and Mushroom Filo Pie

Olive oil
1 small leek, sliced
3–4 rashers lean
    bacon, roughly
    chopped
1 clove garlic,
    crushed
4 mushrooms,
    quartered
150–200g cooked
    chicken, diced
2–3 tablespoons
    crème fraîche or
    natural Greek
    yoghurt
100ml milk
Seasoning to taste
Pinch of tarragon
Pinch of mixed herbs
Approx 30g butter,
    melted
3–5 filo sheets

Note: This is just a
simple recipe – ideal
for using up cooked
chicken from your
Sunday roast!

Whenever I make a pie in the halogen, I only pop pastry on the top as sometimes halogens can give pies an undercooked or soggy bottom unless you bake blind first. I love the texture and simplicity of using filo. No matter how haphazardly you place the filo, it always looks like you have spent hours on the dish.

- In a sauté pan, heat a little olive oil. Add the leek, bacon, garlic and mushrooms and cook until everything starts to soften. Add the chicken and heat thoroughly.
- Add the crème fraîche or yoghurt and the milk. This should give you a nice sauce for the chicken. If you want it to be runnier, you can add more milk, or if you want it to be creamier, add more crème fraîche. Season to taste and add the herbs. Transfer to a deep pie dish.
- Melt the butter in a pan or you could heat it gently in the halogen, but be careful not to burn it.
- Cut each filo sheet into three. Brush each piece with a little butter and screw it up roughly. Press the screwed up pastry onto the top of the pie. Continue until you have filled the top of the pie dish.
- When you are ready to cook, place the dish on the low rack. Turn the temperature to 190°C and cook for 20–30 minutes or until golden on top.
- Serve with mashed potatoes and green vegetables.

CHAPTER 4

Fish

Fish is incredibly healthy, particularly if you opt for oily fish, rich in Omega 3. The halogen is a great tool for cooking fish, especially when foil-baked in its own juices. There are quite a few recipes involving this simple way of cooking as it is not only efficient, but better nutritionally, packing in the flavours, juices and nutrients. The fish that are especially rich in Omega 3 are mackerel, trout, herring, tuna, salmon and sardines. Most of the recipes can be made with a variety of fish, so please experiment.

Foil-baked Salmon with Mango Salsa

2 salmon fillets
2–4 slices of lemon
Lemon juice
Seasoning
½ ripe mango
½ ripe avocado
½ red chilli, finely
   chopped
2–3 spring onions,
   finely chopped
½ yellow pepper,
   diced
Zest and juice of ½
   lime
Generous handful of
   rocket, lamb's leaf,
   watercress or mixed
   leaf salad leaves
½ cucumber, diced
Small handful
   chopped coriander

- Preheat the halogen oven to 190°C.
- Place each salmon fillet in the centre of a piece of foil. Add one or two slices of lemon on top. Finish with a squeeze of extra lemon juice and season to taste. Wrap and place on the medium rack. Cook for 15–20 minutes or to your own personal taste.
- Meanwhile, place the salsa ingredients (all remaining ingredients apart from the salad leaves, cucumber and coriander) together in a bowl and mash/mix well.
- Just prior to serving, place the salad leaves and coriander on the plates. Place the salmon on top and drizzle with salsa. Serve with the remaining half lime on the side.

Crunchy-topped Salmon

- In a bowl, mix the spring onion, breadcrumbs, oats, cornflakes and optional parmesan. Add the natural yoghurt to help bind. Season to taste.
- Place the salmon fillets on a greased baking tray. Carefully spoon over the mixture to form a generous layer on top of the fillets. Press down firmly.
- Place on the middle rack and set the temperature to 190°C. Cook for 10–15 minutes until golden and the fish is cooked to your specification.
- Serve immediately.

2–3 spring onions, finely chopped
30g wholemeal breadcrumbs
20g oats
15g (1 tablespoon) cornflakes, crushed
20g parmesan, grated (optional)
2–3 tablespoons natural yoghurt
Black pepper

Creamy Smoked Haddock Pots

2 smoked haddock
fillets
20g butter
1 small leek, finely
chopped
Black pepper
150ml milk
150g cream cheese
with herbs
50g wholemeal
breadcrumbs
30g parmesan
cheese, grated

These are simple to make and can be prepared in advance and kept in the fridge until needed. If you don't want to serve in individual ramekin dishes, you can prepare the mixture in one larger ovenproof dish.

- Place the smoked haddock fillets on a browning tray, turn the halogen on to 200°C and cook for 6 minutes.
- Meanwhile, melt the butter in a sauté pan. Add the chopped leek and cook until soft. Season with black pepper before adding the milk and cream cheese.
- When the fish is cooked, flake off into the sauté pan.
- Transfer the mixture into ramekin dishes or a larger ovenproof dish. Level off the top.
- Mix the breadcrumbs and parmesan. Season with black pepper. Sprinkle this over the fish mixture.
- Place the dish(es) on the medium rack and cook for 10 minutes at 200°C until golden.

Salmon and Herb Butter Parcels

- Mix the butter and herbs to form a herb butter.
- Cut out two squares of foil, double thickness, big enough to parcel the fillets. Place the fillets on the foil and cover with a layer of herb butter, a slice or two of lemon and a dessertspoon of water. Drizzle with a dash of olive oil and season with black pepper.
- Preheat the halogen oven using the preheat setting or set the temperature to 220°C.
- Seal the foil parcels and place them on a baking tray or directly on the medium rack. Cook for 15–20 minutes until the fish is tender and flaking.
- Serve with new potatoes and green vegetables.

1 tablespoon butter
Small handful of fresh herbs, finely chopped
2 salmon fillets
½ lemon, sliced
Water
Olive oil
Black pepper

Haddock, Egg and Gruyere Bake

200g haddock fillets, roughly chopped
1–2 hard-boiled eggs, halved or quartered
100ml crème fraîche
75ml milk
60g Gruyere cheese, grated
1–2 teaspoons wholegrain mustard
Seasoning
1–2 tablespoons breadcrumbs
1 tablespoon oats
30g parmesan cheese, grated

This is a quick and easy dish and perfect for a comforting supper.

- In an ovenproof dish, making sure it fits in the oven, place the chopped haddock and hard-boiled eggs.
- In a bowl, mix the crème fraîche, milk, grated Gruyere and mustard. Season to taste. Spoon this over the egg and haddock mixture.
- Mix the breadcrumbs, oats and parmesan together, season well and sprinkle over the crème fraîche mixture.
- Preheat the halogen oven using the preheat setting or turn on to 180°C. Place the dish on the low rack and bake in the oven for 15–20 minutes, until the haddock is cooked.
- Serve on its own for a simple supper or with salad and new potatoes.

Baked Italian-style Cod in White Wine

SERVES 2

Olive oil
½ red onion, sliced
1 tomato, sliced
2 cod fillets
4 sundried tomatoes
in oil, drained
4–6 basil leaves
Seasoning to taste
4 tablespoons white
wine

- Cut out two squares of foil, double thickness, big enough to parcel the fillets. Brush the centre of each foil square with olive oil before adding a couple of slices of onion and then a couple of slices of tomato.
- Lay the fish on top of the onion and tomato. Place 2 sundried tomatoes on each fillet, followed by 2 or 3 basil leaves. Season to taste.
- Pull the sides of the foil up to form a bowl shape, ready to add the wine before scrunching securely. Once secure, place on a baking tray. You can leave the fish to marinate until you are ready to cook, or cook it immediately.
- Place on the medium rack and set the halogen to 200°C. Cook for 20 minutes until the fish is tender and flaking.
- Serve with new potatoes and seasonal vegetables.

Note: For extra variety, why not add some pancetta as an extra layer.

Salmon and Fennel Parcels

Olive oil
2 salmon fillets
½ fennel bulb, finely
  sliced
Seasoning to taste
4–6 tablespoons
  white wine or
  vermouth

- Cut out two squares of foil, double thickness, big enough to parcel the fillets. Brush the centre of each foil square with olive oil and lay a fillet on top. Sprinkle with the sliced fennel and season to taste.
- Pull the sides of the foil up to form a bowl shape, ready for the wine to be added. Scrunch securely and place on a baking tray.
- You can leave the salmon to marinate until you are ready to cook it, or cook it immediately. Place on the medium rack and set the halogen to 200°C. Cook for 20 minutes until the fish is tender and flaking.
- Serve with new potatoes and seasonal vegetables.

Salmon, Garlic and White Wine Parcels

This dish takes only minutes to make and can be prepared in advance.

- Put the garlic, honey, mustard, white wine and lemon zest into a bowl and combine well.
- Cut out two squares of foil, double thickness, big enough to parcel the fillets. Butter the foil and add the sliced onion rings. Place the salmon over the onion.
- Spread the garlic sauce over the salmon fillets, ensuring they are coated. Add a sprinkle of dill and season to taste.
- Parcel up the salmon fillets, making sure the edges are sealed well.
- Preheat the halogen oven using the preheat setting or set the temperature to 200°C. Place on the low rack and cook for 15–20 minutes until the fish flakes easily.
- Unwrap and serve with new potatoes and green vegetables.

1–2 cloves of garlic, crushed
2 teaspoons honey
1–2 teaspoons wholegrain mustard
2 tablespoons white wine
Zest of 1 lemon
Butter
1 small onion, sliced into rings
2 salmon fillets
Small handful of fresh dill, finely chopped
Seasoning to taste

Baked Trout with Creamy Lemon and Dill

SERVES 2

2 rainbow trout fillets
Olive oil
Black pepper
2 cloves of garlic,
  sliced
½ chilli, finely
  chopped
½ pepper, finely
  chopped
Lemon juice
Dessertspoon freshly
  chopped dill
2–4 dessertspoons
  natural yoghurt

- Rub the fillets with olive oil and season with black pepper.
- Cut out two sheets of foil big enough to parcel up each fillet. Lay the fish on top and place the garlic, chilli and pepper on the fish.
- Mix the lemon juice (to taste), dill and yoghurt together. Season to taste. Place 1–2 dessertspoons on each fillet.
- Fold the foil up to form a secure parcel and place on the middle rack. Set the temperature to 200°C and bake for 15–20 minutes.
- Serve with new potatoes and fresh seasonal greens.

One-pot Cod

- Place the bacon, mushrooms and onion in a greased ovenproof dish. Don't choose a dish that is too large – it should be big enough to hold the fillets, but not so big that the ingredients become a bit lost. Drizzle sparingly with olive oil.
- Butter one side of each fillet before placing them, buttered-side up, onto the bacon mixture. Season well with sea salt and black pepper.
- Finally, drizzle over the white wine before covering with a double layer of tin foil, held securely.
- Place the dish on the medium rack and cook at 200°C for 20 minutes.
- Uncover and cook for a further 5 minutes before serving with new potatoes and green seasonal vegetables.

50–75g lean, thick bacon, cut into chunks
50g button mushrooms, halved
1 small onion, finely chopped
Olive oil
2 cod fillets
25g butter
Sea salt
Black pepper
200ml white wine

Tuna and Sweetcorn Lasagne

200g tuna (roughly 1 tin), mashed

2–3 spring onions, chopped

100g sweetcorn (tinned or frozen)

Seasoning to taste

Lasagne sheets

250ml passata

Parmesan or other cheese for topping, grated

Black pepper

- Mix the tuna, spring onion and sweetcorn together in a bowl. Season to taste.
- Add a layer of tuna mash to the bottom of a small lasagne dish, cover with a layer of lasagne sheets and top with a layer of passata. Continue this process once more, ending with a layer of passata.
- Preheat the halogen oven using the preheat setting or set the temperature to 210°C.
- Grate parmesan or other cheese over the final layer of passata and sprinkle with black pepper.
- Place on the medium rack and cook for 30–40 minutes, until golden and the pasta sheets are cooked. If the top starts to get too dark, cover with tin foil, making sure it is secure. (The cooking time can be greatly reduced if you use fresh lasagne sheets.)
- Serve with salad and garlic bread.

Simple Baked Mackerel

SERVES 2

Simple dishes are often the best. Serve this with a green salad and new potatoes for a quick and easy supper.

- Cover the middle rack of your halogen with foil, making sure it is secure by folding it under. Brush with oil or butter to help prevent the fish from sticking.
- Place the fish onto the rack skin-side up and brush with olive oil. Season with sea salt and black pepper and a squeeze of lemon juice if preferred.
- Bake at 210°C until the skin is brown. Turn the fish over and brush again with olive oil and season. Cook for another 5 minutes.
- Drizzle with lemon juice and serve.

2 mackerel fillets
Olive oil (I use oils flavoured with garlic or chilli to add more flavour)
Sea salt
Black pepper
Lemon juice

Honeyed Salmon and Asparagus Parcels

10g butter
2 tablespoons runny honey
1 tablespoon Dijon mustard
Zest of ½ lemon
Seasoning to taste
2 salmon fillets
250g fresh asparagus, trimmed

My mum passed on this recipe, which is truly delicious and so simple. Yes it is another parcel recipe but really, why not? They are so easy to make and save on washing up – what's not to like? Try to buy asparagus when in season – the taste of fresh British asparagus is second to none.

- Melt the butter and mix with the honey, mustard and lemon zest. Season to taste.
- Prepare two squares of doubled-up foil, big enough to parcel the fish. Place the asparagus on each square, followed by the salmon. Drizzle with the honey mixture. Seal the foil parcels securely.
- Turn the halogen oven to 210°C. Place the parcels on the middle rack and cook for 20–25 minutes or until the fish flakes easily.
- Serve with new potatoes and green seasonal vegetables.

Simple Foil-baked Herrings

SERVES 2

- Scale and wash the herrings ready to cook. Place each one on a piece of greased foil, large enough to parcel the fish.
- Place a spoonful of butter onto each herring, spreading it out roughly. Add the lemon zest and a generous squeeze of lemon juice. Season with sea salt and black pepper to taste.
- Wrap the foil securely and place on the medium rack. Turn the temperature to 190°C and cook for 15–20 minutes until the fish is cooked to your requirements and flakes off easily with a fork.
- Serve with new potatoes and fresh seasonal salad.

2 herrings, filleted
2 teaspoons butter
Zest and juice of 1
  lemon
Sea salt
Black pepper

Creamy Haddock Gratin

2–4 haddock fillets, depending on appetite
1 dessertspoon butter
1 small onion, finely sliced
Sea salt
Black pepper
175g crème fraîche or Total Greek yoghurt (use double cream if you don't mind the calories!)
100ml milk
Zest and juice of ½ lemon
1–2 teaspoons wholegrain mustard
50g oats
50g wholemeal breadcrumbs
30g freshly grated parmesan

- Wash the fish fillets before spreading a thin layer of butter on one side of each. Place them buttered-side down in a greased ovenproof dish. Cover with the onion and season with sea salt and black pepper.
- In a bowl, mix the crème fraîche or yoghurt with the milk, lemon zest, juice and mustard. Pour this over the fish, spreading until covered.
- In a bowl, mix the oats, breadcrumbs and parmesan. Sprinkle this evenly over the creamy mixture.
- Place on the medium rack and turn the temperature to 190°C. Cook for 20 minutes until golden and bubbling and the fish is cooked to your requirements.
- Serve with new potatoes and seasonal vegetables or on its own for a simple supper.

Note: For variation, you could add a thickly sliced hard-boiled egg over the onion slices, before adding the creamy mixture.

Easy Pesto Salmon

This really is a simple dish. Try to remember to marinate for at least 1 hour, but ideally 3–4 hours before cooking as this really improves the flavour.

- Place the fish fillets in a freezer bag. Add the white wine, lemon juice and zest. Season to taste with black pepper. Seal, shake well and leave in the fridge to marinate.
- When ready to cook, turn the halogen to high (240–250°C) as you are going to grill the salmon.
- Remove the salmon from the bag and place on a greased baking tray. Spread the pesto over the top of each fillet. Finish with a sprinkle of fresh breadcrumbs.
- Place on the middle rack and cook for 10 minutes or until the fish is done to your requirements. You should be able to flake the fish with a fork.
- Serve immediately.

2 salmon fillets
3 tablespoons white wine or vermouth
Zest and juice of ½ lemon
Black pepper
2–3 tablespoons pesto
1 tablespoon wholemeal breadcrumbs

One-pot Roasted Fish, Fennel and Red Onion

SERVES 2

2–4 white fish fillets, depending on appetite

1 small fennel bulb, sliced

1 red onion, sliced

1–2 cloves of garlic, finely sliced

1 lemon, cut into wedges

Juice of 1 lemon

Olive oil

Butter

Seasoning to taste

- Season the fish fillets well and squeeze over a little lemon juice. Leave to one side until needed.
- Preheat the halogen oven using the preheat setting or set the temperature to 220°C.
- Place the sliced fennel, onion, garlic and lemon wedges into a roasting or baking tray, making sure it fits in your halogen.
- Drizzle with olive oil and place in the oven on the low rack for 15 minutes.
- Place the fish fillets on top of the vegetables. Place a small knob of butter on each fillet. Drizzle the juice of 1 lemon over the dish. Season to taste and cover securely with foil. Bake for another 15–20 minutes until the fish is thoroughly cooked and flakes easily off the fork.
- Remove the foil and serve with new potatoes and a fresh green salad.

Salmon, Honey and Mustard Crusts

Simple yet delicious

- Squeeze the lemon juice over the salmon fillets.
- Mix the mustard and honey together. In another bowl, mix the breadcrumbs and cornflakes together.
- Spread the mustard coating on the fillets ensuring the tops are well coated. Then dip them into the breadcrumb mixture, again ensuring they are well coated.
- Preheat the halogen oven using the preheat setting or set the temperature to 200°C.
- Place the fillets on a baking tray on the medium rack. Cook for 12–15 minutes until the fillets are cooked.
- Serve with a green salad and new potatoes.

SERVES 2

2 salmon fillets
Juice of ½ lemon
1–2 tablespoons wholegrain mustard
1–2 tablespoons honey
1 tablespoon wholemeal breadcrumbs
1 tablespoon cornflakes, crushed (if you don't have cornflakes, use finely chopped nuts)

Salmon Fish Cakes

200g fresh or tinned
salmon
200g potatoes,
cooked and
mashed
1–2 teaspoons lemon
juice
1 teaspoon each of
fresh dill and
tarragon (or ½
teaspoon each of
dried)
1 egg, beaten
Olive oil

- Mix the fish, potato, lemon juice and herbs together in a bowl. Add the egg to bind.
- Form the mixture into cakes, place on baking parchment and chill in the fridge for 10 minutes.
- Preheat the halogen oven using the preheat setting or set the temperature to 250°C.
- Remove the fish cakes from the fridge and brush with a light coating of olive oil.
- Place on the high rack either on a baking tray or a browning pan, or you can place them directly on the rack. Cook the cakes for 5–6 minutes each side, turning halfway through to ensure they are evenly cooked and browned. (You are actually grilling them at this heat.)
- Serve with new potatoes and a green salad.

Mackerel and Cider Parcels

Yet another foil parcel but, really, the halogen is made for this type of recipe and they are so very easy. You can also prepare the parcels in advance, leaving them to marinate in the fridge.

- Wash the fillets. Cut two pieces of foil, large enough to parcel each fillet, and grease the centre of each with butter.
- Place the red onion slices on each piece of foil. Place the mackerel on top, followed by a slice of lemon.
- Pull the sides of the foil up as if you are ready to seal, which will prevent the cider from escaping. Then add the cider, parsley, and season with black pepper and sea salt. Close the parcel securely.
- When you are ready to cook, place the parcels on the medium rack and set the temperature to 200°C. Cook for 15–20 minutes until done to your requirements.
- Serve with green salad and new potatoes.

2 mackerel fillets (or 2 small whole mackerel, filleted)
Butter
1 small red onion, sliced
2 thick slices of lemon
2–4 tablespoons cider
Small handful of freshly chopped parsley
Black pepper
Sea salt

Italian Style Tuna & Mushroom Bakes

2 large portobello or
flat mushrooms
Olive oil
1 clove of garlic,
finely crushed
1 small red onion,
finely chopped
2 tomatoes, finely
chopped
4-5 leaves of basil,
finely chopped
75g tuna, mashed
30-40g feta, crumbled
Black pepper
Sea salt
Sprinkle of parmesan

- Wash the mushrooms. Brush them with olive oil and sprinkle with a little garlic.
- Place on the high rack on a browning tray. Turn the temperature to 180°C and cook for 8 minutes.
- Meanwhile combine the remaining ingredients apart from the parmesan. Season to taste.
- When the mushrooms have finished cooking, place the mixture in the centre, stuffing them well. Finish with a sprinkle of parmesan.
- Place back on the high rack and cook for a further 10–15 minutes until soft and golden.
- Serve with green salad.

Haddock Fishcakes

- Cook and mash the potatoes until they are light and fluffy. Add the flaked/chopped haddock, spring onions and the egg and combine well.
- Add the chopped parsley. Season to taste.
- Roll into balls before flattening into cakes. Place each cake on a greased browning tray. Brush with olive oil.
- When ready to cook, place on the high rack and cook at 230°C, turning occasionally until cooked to perfection.
- Serve with green salad.

350g potatoes, cooked and mashed
100g haddock, skinned, boned and chopped
4 spring onions, finely chopped,
1 egg, beaten
Sea salt
Black pepper
Small handful chopped parsley
Olive oil

Cheesy Fish Crumble

225g white fish
300ml milk
1 bay leaf
Sea salt
Black pepper
Olive oil
50g butter
1 small onion, finely
    chopped
1 small leek, trimmed
    and sliced
1 small carrot, peeled
    and chopped into
    small pieces
1 large potato,
    peeled and cut into
    small pieces
80g plain flour
150ml fish or
    vegetable stock
½ teaspoon dried dill

Crumble topping:
50g butter
75g plain flour
50g grated parmesan
    cheese
½ teaspoon mustard
    powder

- Place the fish in a pan with the milk, bay leaf and seasoning to taste. Bring to the boil and cook for 8–10 minutes until tender.
- Remove the fish from the milk, keeping the milk for later. Gently flake the fish into a greased ovenproof dish.
- Put a dash of olive oil and half the butter into a sauté pan. Gently cook the vegetables for 2 minutes before adding a lid. Reduce the heat to low and cook gently for 10–15 minutes.
- Meanwhile, melt the remaining butter in a saucepan, add the flour and cook for 1 minute, stirring continually with a wooden spoon. Add the remaining milk and stock, and continue to stir until it starts to thicken.
- Remove from the heat, season to taste and add the dill. Pour the sauce over the fish.
- To make the topping, simply rub the butter and the flour together (it will look like breadcrumbs). Stir in the cheese and the mustard powder. Season to taste. Scatter this over the fish mixture.
- Place on the medium rack and set the temperature to 190°C. Cook for 15–20 minutes until golden and bubbling.
- Serve with green vegetables.

CHAPTER 5

Vegetarian

You don't have to be a vegetarian to enjoy
vegetarian food. Nutritionally I would advise
people to have at least two meatfree days a
week. A diet rich in fresh, wholesome
vegetables, fruit, nuts and seeds, along with
oily fish is really what we should all strive for.
This chapter contains some simple dishes
which should appeal to all tastes. Cheese and
eggs do appear frequently simply because that
is what people love, but if you are watching
your weight and cholesterol levels, try to cut
down on the cheese consumption. There are
many half fat/low fat Cheddars on the market
now which work really well in most recipes,
and taste-wise there is really no difference.

Goat's Cheese and Sundried Tomato Tower

SERVES 2

2 portobello
    mushrooms (or large
    flat mushrooms)
Garlic-infused olive oil
100g goat's cheese
Black pepper to taste
2 generous handfuls
    of a selection of
    salad leaves (ideally
    rocket, watercress,
    spinach with lettuce
    leaves)
¼ cucumber, diced into
    3–4 inch chunks
½ red pepper, diced
2–3 spring onions,
    chopped
½ green apple, diced
½ orange, peeled and
    sliced
8–10 cherry
    tomatoes, halved
25g toasted pine nuts
    or seeds
2 slices of ciabatta
    bread
4–6 sundried tomatoes
    (in oil, drained)
Drizzle of balsamic
    vinegar
Drizzle of sweet chilli
    sauce

Not so much a tower I suppose, but definitely an eye-catching and very, very tasty dish. This recipe takes a maximum of 15 minutes from the start of preparation until you sit down to eat. It also has the look of a very professional dish – excellent for a quick and tasty supper or reduce the quantities and make it a dinner party starter.

- Wash the mushrooms, remove the stalks and brush with the garlic-infused olive oil. Fill the cup of each mushroom with goat's cheese. Season with black pepper. Place on the high rack and cook at 220°C for 8 minutes.
- While that is cooking, place the salad leaves on two dinner plates. On top of the leaves, sprinkle the cucumber, pepper, spring onions, apple, orange slices, cherry tomatoes and pine nuts.
- When the halogen beeps, add the ciabatta slices to the high rack and continue to cook for another 3–4 minutes.
- When ready, place the ciabatta in the centre of each dinner plate. Place the mushroom over the bread, followed by 2–3 sundried tomatoes.
- Finish with a drizzle of balsamic vinegar and sweet chilli sauce. Serve immediately.

Muffin Pizzas

This really is a simple, cheat dish but yummy, especially when served with a lovely bed of salad as given in the recipe opposite.

- Place the sliced muffins on your worktop and spread with the pasta sauce.
- Add your choice of topping and end with a coating of grated cheese. Finish with a sprinkle of oregano and seasoning to taste.
- Place on the high rack and cook at 220°C for 8–10 minutes until golden.
- Serve immediately.

1–2 muffins, sliced in half horizontally
2–4 teaspoons pasta sauce
Pizza topping of your choice, e.g.
Red onion, goat's cheese and spinach leaves
Mozzarella and tomato
Pepperoni
Ham and pineapple
Cheese, grated (e.g. mature Cheddar, mozzarella, parmesan)
Dried oregano
Seasoning to taste

Veggie Yorkshire

1 small red onion,
   cut into wedges
2–3 cloves of garlic,
   halved
½ red pepper, cut
   into wedges
8 cherry or vine
   tomatoes, left
   whole
Olive oil
Balsamic vinegar
   (optional)
Sugar
Black pepper
Sea salt
Sprigs of thyme
50g plain flour
150ml milk
1 egg

Yorkshire puddings are so easy to make. Stuff them with roasted vegetables and serve with roast potatoes for a delicious meal.

- In an ovenproof dish (this will also finally hold the Yorkshire mixture), place the vegetables and finish with a drizzle of olive oil, a dash of balsamic (optional) and a tiny sprinkle of sugar. Season with black pepper and sea salt and add the thyme sprigs. Place on the medium rack and cook for 20 minutes at 200°C.
- While that is cooking, beat the flour, milk and egg together until you have a smooth batter. Place this in the fridge until needed.
- When the vegetables are done, leave them in the oven but spread them evenly in the dish. Immediately pour the batter onto the vegetables and shut the halogen lid. Cook at 210°C for 20 minutes until risen and golden.
- Serve immediately.

Warm Beetroot Salad

This recipe is truly delicious.

- Place the cubed root vegetables (all cut to a similar size) in a tin or browning tray. Drizzle with olive oil, ensuring the vegetables are all evenly coated. Sprinkle with oregano, sea salt, black pepper and a drizzle of balsamic.
- Place on the middle rack and set the temperature to 210°C. Cook for 20 minutes, or until soft and sweet.
- Meanwhile, place the salad leaves in your serving dishes. Add the chopped red onion (or spring onions) and the red pepper. Toss to ensure everything is evenly distributed.
- When the vegetables are cooked, simply place in them in the centre of your salad, finishing with a sprinkle of feta or goat's cheese.
- Serve immediately.

1–2 beetroots, peeled and cubed
1–2 parsnips, peeled and cubed
1 small sweet potato, peeled and cubed
Olive oil
¼ teaspoon dried oregano
Sea salt
Black pepper
Balsamic vinegar
2 handfuls of seasonal salad leaves, washed
1 small red onion, sliced (or 4–5 spring onions, sliced)
½ red pepper, sliced
50g feta or soft goat's cheese

Cheese and Herb Soufflés

25g butter
20g plain flour
75ml milk
125g ricotta cheese
15g parmesan
  cheese, grated
2 eggs, separated
1 additional egg
  white
Handful of fresh
  herbs, chopped
  (such as parsley,
  thyme, chives,
  oregano or
  rosemary)

I know you are probably thinking, soufflés are not quick and easy, but really, they are. We all fear soufflés, but with practice, they really can be straightforward. Give them a try and, you know what they say, practice makes perfect.

- To start the soufflés, make a roux, which is a basic start to a white sauce. Melt the butter in a pan and add the flour, stirring well using a wooden spoon to avoid lumps. Add the milk and change to a balloon whisk (this helps avoid lumps). Cook until the sauce thickens and then remove from the heat.
- Add the ricotta and parmesan cheese, before adding the 2 egg yolks, herbs and seasoning.
- In a clean bowl (this should not have any grease on it or the egg white won't fluff up), add the 3 egg whites. Beat until the mixture forms stiff peaks. Once achieved, fold in a spoonful of the ricotta mixture as this will help loosen the egg whites and help you combine the rest of the mixture.
- When you have done this, you can then add the egg whites to the rest of the cheese mixture and fold carefully. Don't over-fold or they could go flat.
- Grease your soufflé dishes and pour in the mixture until it reaches the top.

- Preheat the halogen oven using the preheat setting or set the temperature to 180°C.
- Place the soufflés in a deep tray, making sure it fits in your halogen oven. Fill the tray with hot water until it reaches halfway up the soufflé dishes.
- Place on the medium rack and cook for 20–25 minutes until the soufflés are firm, risen and golden but have a soft centre.
- Serve immediately before they slump.

Spicy Roasted Sweet Potato with Yoghurt Dressing

1 sweet potato, evenly diced
1 red onion, quartered
1–2 cloves of garlic, roughly chopped
Drizzle of olive oil
½ chilli
2–3cm knuckle of fresh ginger
1 teaspoon coriander seeds
1 teaspoon cumin seeds
½ teaspoon turmeric
Seasoning
Small handful of fresh coriander leaves, chopped
1–2 tablespoons thick yoghurt (I prefer using a Greek yoghurt such as Total)

- Turn on your halogen oven to 200°C.
- In an ovenproof dish, add the sweet potato (making sure it is evenly diced), onion and garlic, and coat/toss well in the olive oil. Place on the low rack and cook for 10 minutes.
- Meanwhile, chop the chilli, grate the ginger and crush the coriander, cumin and turmeric. Mix together thoroughly. Season to taste.
- Once the sweet potato has cooked for 10 minutes, lift the halogen lid and sprinkle the spices over the vegetables. Carefully toss again, ensuring it is all well covered. If necessary you can add a little more oil but it should not be soaked in oil – just lightly covered.
- Turn the halogen back on to 200°C and cook for another 15–20 minutes until the potato is soft.
- Then remove and place in a serving dish. Add the chopped coriander leaves and serve with a dollop of yoghurt.

Italian-style Devilled Mushrooms

This is a lovely starter or snack – simple to make but tastes delicious. For extra yumminess, add some crumbled goat's cheese over the mushrooms during the last 5 minutes of baking.

- In a bowl, mix together all the ingredients apart from the mushrooms.
- Place the mushrooms on a greased baking tray and cover with the paste. Cover the tray with clingfilm and place in the fridge to marinate for at least 1 hour.
- When you are ready to cook, heat the halogen to 200°C. Place the tray on the medium rack and cook for 8–10 minutes or until the mushrooms are cooked to your satisfaction.
- Serve on a bed of green salad.

1–2 tablespoons sundried tomato purée
1 teaspoon wholegrain mustard
2 cloves of garlic, crushed
1 tablespoon olive oil
2 sprigs of fresh thyme, finely chopped
Sea salt
Black pepper
2–4 large mushrooms (depending on appetite)

1–2 fennel bulbs, cut
  into wedges
Olive oil
1–2 cloves of garlic,
  chopped
Sea salt
Black pepper

Baked Fennel

Fennel is a really under-rated vegetable. It has a lovely flavour and goes well with fish dishes as well as vegetarian or meat dishes. This is a very simple side dish.

- Place the fennel in a pan of boiling water and simmer gently for 10 minutes. Drain and place in an oiled ovenproof dish.
- Drizzle with olive oil and add the chopped garlic. Season with sea salt and black pepper.
- Place on the medium rack and set the temperature to 190°C. Cook for 20–25 minutes.
- Serve with a drizzle of extra virgin olive oil.

Mediterranean-style pasta bake

- Place the dried pasta in a pan of boiling water and cook as per the manufacturer's instructions.
- Meanwhile, in a sauté pan, heat a dash of olive oil and add the onion, garlic, courgette and red pepper. Cook until they start to soften before adding the chopped tomatoes and thyme. Season to taste. If you like a richer sauce you might want to add a dash or two of red wine.
- Drain the pasta and add to the vegetable mixture. Combine well before placing in an ovenproof dish. Sprinkle with parmesan.
- Set the halogen oven to 220°C. Place the dish on the medium rack and cook until golden and bubbling – this should only take 5 minutes or so.
- Serve immediately with crusty bread and a salad.

150g penne pasta
Olive oil
1 small red onion, finely chopped
2 cloves of garlic, roughly chopped
1 courgette, sliced
½ red pepper, diced
200g chopped tomatoes
1–2 sprigs of thyme
Black pepper
Sea salt
Red wine (optional)
10–20g parmesan, grated

Goat's Cheese, Broccoli and Tomato Tart

100g plain flour
50g cold butter
100g crème fraîche
70ml milk
2 eggs, 1 beaten, 1
  separated
Seasoning to taste
Handful of fresh
  herbs (parsley,
  oregano or chives)
60g goat's cheese
75g broccoli, cooked
100g cherry
  tomatoes, halved

This is a really lovely quiche-style tart and perfect for using up any leftovers. I adore the taste of goat's cheese in cooking but if you don't fancy it, why don't you opt for a strong mature cheese instead? The halogen is not the best oven for pastry bases, so I would strongly advise following the instructions and pre-baking the pastry case. This recipe will line a small flan tin.

• In a bowl, add the flour and the cold butter. Using your fingertips, rub until the butter mixes with the flour. It should look a bit like breadcrumbs. Add a little cold water until you form a firm but not too wet dough. Wrap this in clingfilm and place in the fridge to rest for half an hour.

• When the pastry is ready to roll, lightly dust your work surface with flour. Press the dough into a flat circle, dusting top and bottom to ensure it does not stick. With even strokes, roll the pastry a few times then turn clockwise – this will ensure you maintain the circle for your tin. When ready, fold the end of the circle over your rolling pin and roll slightly to gather up the pastry. Unroll over the tin and press down firmly around the edges and base.

- Prick with a fork before lining with parchment and covering with baking beans. (You could use dried pulses such as chickpeas or even rice if you don't have any baking beans.)
- Place in the halogen on the middle rack. Set the temperature to 190°C and cook for 15 minutes.
- Remove the baking beans and bake for another 5–10 minutes until cooked. Remove from the oven.
- In a jug, beat the crème fraîche with the milk and 1 whole egg. Separate the remaining egg and add the yolk to the crème fraîche. Brush the pastry case with the egg white – this helps prevent the mixture making the pastry too wet. Then add the remaining egg white to the crème fraîche. Season the crème fraîche mixture with black pepper, salt and a handful of fresh herbs if you prefer.
- Place the goat's cheese, broccoli and tomatoes in the pastry case. Pour the crème fraîche mixture over the vegetables.
- Place back onto the medium rack and cook at 170°C for 30 minutes or until set and golden.
- Serve hot or cold.

Cheesy Egg Gratin

SERVES 2

4 eggs
10g butter
15g plain flour or cornflour
300ml milk
30–60g mature Cheddar, grated (depending on taste)
Black pepper
Sea salt
¼ teaspoon mustard (optional)
2 tomatoes, sliced
2 tablespoons oats
2 tablespoons breadcrumbs
1 tablespoon mature Cheddar or parmesan, grated

I used to have this when I was a child and it is surprisingly filling and comforting – a great, tasty supper. Simple to prepare, this dish can be made in advance and heated in the halogen. The cheats could buy readymade cheese sauce, or mix crème fraîche with mature cheddar and a little milk, but for me there is nothing like the taste of a fresh, traditional cheese sauce.

- Place the eggs in boiling water and cook them for 10 minutes until they are hard-boiled. Alternatively, you could actually hard-boil the eggs in the halogen. To do this, place the eggs in the halogen egg rack and set the temperature to 180°C. Cook for 10 minutes or until they are ready. Take care removing the eggs from the halogen as they can be very hot.
- While the eggs are cooking, start to prepare the cheese sauce. In a heavy-based saucepan on a medium heat, melt the butter and then add the flour. Using a wooden spoon, mix the butter and flour to form a paste-like dough. Add a little milk at a time and continue to stir. If lumps begin to develop in the sauce, switch to a balloon whisk and beat well. This will ensure a lovely smooth sauce. Add the cheese and continue to stir until it has melted and you are left with a glossy sauce.

- Once thickened, season with black pepper and sea salt and add the mustard.
- Shell the hard-boiled eggs and halve them. Place in the bottom of an ovenproof dish. Pour the cheese on top and add the tomato slices.
- Mix the oats, breadcrumbs and tablespoon of cheese together, season and sprinkle this over the tomatoes.
- Place on the medium rack and set the temperature to 220°C. Cook until golden and bubbling – this should only take 5–8 minutes. If you are cooking this as a pre-prepared dish from cold, reduce the temperature to 200°C and cook for 15 minutes.

Tomato and Mozzarella Puff Tarts

SERVES 2

¼ pack of readymade puff pastry

2 teaspoons sundried tomato paste

½ pack of mozzarella

Handful of basil leaves

4–5 cherry tomatoes

Seasoning to taste

Extra basil leaves to garnish

Puff pastry is the busy cook's best friend. You can create your own toppings but this is a simple favourite to help get you started.

- Roll out the pastry to a 2–3mm thickness. Cut into 2–3 squares. Carefully score around the edge of each square with a knife, 1cm from the edge of the pastry – do not cut the pastry, just make a slight indent.
- Preheat the halogen oven using the preheat setting or turn on to 210°C.
- In the middle of each square add a teaspoon of sundried tomato paste and spread evenly within the scored line. Place pieces of mozzarella and a few leaves of basil inside the scored line. Add a few cherry tomatoes, halved or whole, depending on your preference. Season to taste.
- Place on the high rack and bake in the oven for about 15 minutes until the pastry is golden. If the tarts start to brown before the base is cooked, transfer to the low rack for a few more minutes.
- Before serving, add a garnish of basil leaves.

Simple Mushroom Bake

- Flatten the bread slices with a rolling pin and roll them out as thinly as you can. Place each piece of bread into a 10cm (4in) tartlet tin, leaving the bread extending up the sides of the tin. Place on the medium rack of your halogen and set the temperature to 190°C. Bake for 8–10 minutes, then remove and place to one side.
- In a sauté pan, melt a small knob of butter. Add the mushrooms and garlic and cook until the mushrooms start to soften. Remove the mushrooms from the pan with a slotted spoon and transfer to a heatproof dish. Cover with a lid or foil and place into the oven to keep warm – set the temperature to 120°C.
- Add the mustard and stock to the pan. Reduce the juices in the pan, by cooking for 2–3 minutes, until the sauce thickens.
- Remove from the heat. Season and add the chopped parsley and crème fraîche. Combine well.
- Remove the mushrooms from the oven. Place the bread cases on plates and share the mushroom mixture between them, spoon over the sauce and garnish with the chopped chives.
- Serve immediately with a large green salad.

2 slices of white bread (crusts removed)
Butter
100g of sliced mushrooms (a mixture of oyster and chestnut is good)
1 clove of garlic, crushed
½ teaspoon mustard
150ml vegetable stock
Black pepper
Sea salt
Small handful of freshly chopped parsley
1 tablespoon crème fraîche
Snipped chives to garnish

Vegetable Mornay Bake

1 carrot
1 small leek
½ small head of
   broccoli
½ small cauliflower
10g butter
10g plain flour or
   cornflour
250–300ml milk
1 tablespoon
   nutritional yeast
   flakes (optional)
60g mature cheese,
   grated
¼ teaspoon mustard
   (optional)
Black pepper
1 tablespoon oats
1 tablespoon home-
   prepared
   wholemeal
   breadcrumbs
20g parmesan cheese

A family favourite, suitable as a main meal or even a side dish. Have a look in your local supermarket as they often sell broccoli and cauliflower florets in a bag which is enough for two people – cheaper than buying whole heads and wasting them.

- Chop the carrot into sticks, slice the leek and cut the broccoli and cauliflower into manageable florets. Place in a steamer and cook until the cauliflower is tender but not soft.
- Meanwhile, make the sauce. Melt the butter gently in a saucepan on a medium heat (not high!). Add the flour or cornflour and stir well with a wooden spoon. Add the milk a little at a time, continuing to stir to avoid lumps.
- Switch now to a balloon whisk. Continue to stir over a medium heat until the sauce begins to thicken. The balloon whisk will also help to eradicate any lumps that may have formed. Add more milk as necessary to get the desired thickness. The sauce should be the thickness of custard.
- If you are using nutritional yeast flakes, add these before the grated cheese as they will reduce the amount of cheese you will need – taste as you go! Add the cheese and mustard and stir well. Season with black pepper.

- When the vegetables are ready, transfer them to an ovenproof dish. Pour on the cheese sauce, ensuring all the vegetables are covered.
- Mix the oats, breadcrumbs and parmesan together thoroughly. Scatter over the cheese sauce.
- Preheat the halogen oven using the preheat setting or set the temperature to 210°C.
- Place the mornay on the low rack. Cook for 15–20 minutes until the top is golden and crispy.

Spinach and Ricotta Lasagne

½ onion, finely
  chopped
½ pot of ricotta
50g mature Cheddar,
  grated
75g fresh spinach
  leaves (baby
  spinach is best)
Grated nutmeg
Black pepper to taste
Lasagne sheets
1 small jar of pasta
  sauce
Grated parmesan or
  other cheese for
  topping

I have had so many compliments about this recipe which appears in other books I have written that I just had to include it here also, altered to serve two. We enjoy this dish at least twice a month. It has some great flavours, so even if you aren't vegetarian give it a try as I am sure it will impress. Unlike most lasagne recipes, this one takes just minutes to prepare. I recommend using *Seeds of Change Cherry Tomato, Basil and Parmesan Pasta Sauce* – it has an authentic homemade taste and look.

- Place the onion, ricotta and Cheddar in a bowl and mix well. Add the spinach leaves. (Placing the spinach in a colander and running it under a hot tap for a few seconds softens the leaves and makes the mixing easier.)
- Once mixed, add some grated nutmeg and season with black pepper.
- Place a thin layer of ricotta mixture in the bottom of a lasagne dish, followed by a layer of lasagne sheets. (If you use fresh lasagne sheets, the cooking time can be halved. Alternatively, you could boil the dried lasagne sheets for a few minutes before using.) Top with a thin layer of pasta sauce. Continue with a layer of ricotta, then lasagne, and finally the remaining pasta sauce. Add approximately 30ml of water to the empty jar, rinse the jar and pour the water over the top of the lasagne.

- Grate some parmesan or other cheese onto the lasagne and season.
- Preheat the halogen oven by selecting the preheat option or set the temperature to 200°C.
- Place the lasagne on the low rack and cook for 35–45 minutes. If the top starts to get too dark, cover with tin foil, making sure it is secure.

Serve with potato wedges and salad – delicious!

Roasted Mixed Vegetables with Garlic Dip

2–3 cloves of garlic, crushed
1 medium onion, cut into thick wedges
2 small carrots, peeled and cut into large batons
1 small parsnip, peeled and cut into large batons
2 medium potatoes, peeled and quartered
¼–½ fennel bulb, sliced thickly
2–3 sprigs of thyme
Sea salt
Black pepper
Olive oil
125g garlic/herb cream cheese
2 tablespoons milk
Zest of ½ lemon

A really simple dish – perfect for friends to dig in and enjoy!

- Place all vegetables and herbs into an ovenproof dish. Season with salt and pepper. Drizzle with olive oil and mix lightly, ensuring everything is evenly distributed.
- Set the halogen to 200°C. Place the dish on the medium rack and bake for 30–40 minutes or until the vegetables are golden and roasted.
- While that is cooking, melt the cream cheese, milk and lemon zest in a pan. Season to taste.
- Place the cooked vegetables onto a serving dish. Pour the sauce into ramekin dishes and place by the dish as a dip. Serve immediately.

Stuffed Tomatoes

SERVES 2

You could use any leftover cooked rice for this dish instead of making fresh rice.

- Place the rice into a saucepan with the stock and bring to the boil. Simmer until tender. Drain and place to one side.
- Place some olive oil in a small pan and fry the onion, garlic, pepper, chilli and mushrooms for 2 minutes.
- Add to the rice with the oregano and seasoning and combine well. Remove from the heat. Stir in the beaten egg and mix again.
- Slice the tops off the tomatoes, but don't discard them. Scoop out the flesh and add this to the rice mixture.
- Sprinkle the sugar into the base of each tomato before filling with the rice mixture.
- Place the tomatoes on a greased baking tray. Add the tomato lids and brush with a little oil (I use garlic oil for this).
- Place on the medium rack and cook at 200°C for 20 minutes.
- Serve immediately with fresh crusty bread and salad.

50g rice
300ml vegetable stock
Olive oil
1 small onion, finely chopped
1 clove of garlic, crushed
½ green or yellow pepper, deseeded and chopped
½ red chilli, deseeded and finely chopped
25g mushrooms, finely chopped
1 teaspoon oregano
Sea salt
Black pepper
1 small egg, beaten
2 large ripe beef tomatoes
1 teaspoon caster sugar

Roasted Vegetable Curry

1 red onion, cut into
wedges
1 sweet potato,
thickly diced
1 potato, thickly
diced
½ small butternut
squash, unpeeled
and cut into 2cm-
thick chunks or
wedges
1 carrot, thickly
sliced
Olive oil
Seasoning
Paprika
½ teaspoon coriander
seeds
½ teaspoon cumin
seeds
½ red chilli
2 cloves garlic
½in knuckle of ginger
1 teaspoon turmeric
1 teaspoon garam
masala
Small handful of
coriander leaves
3–4 spring onions
200–300ml water

I adore curries and roasted vegetables so why not put the two together. It creates a very simple curry dish that tastes fantastic.

- Preheat the halogen oven using the preheat setting or set the temperature to 220°C.
- Prepare your vegetables. Place the red onion, potatoes, butternut squash and carrot in an ovenproof dish (making sure it fits in your halogen). Drizzle with olive oil and a sprinkle of seasoning and paprika and toss until combined, ensuring the vegetables are evenly coated in oil. Place the vegetables on the high rack and cook for 20 minutes.
- Meanwhile, place the coriander seeds and cumin seeds in a dry, large sauté pan and heat gently for 1–2 minutes. When the fragrance starts to break through, crush the warmed seeds in a pestle and mortar and combine. Leave the sauté pan to one side, as you will need this in a moment.
- In your liquidiser, add the spices, chilli, garlic, ginger, turmeric, garam masala, coriander leaves, spring onions and seasoning. Combine well. Add olive oil until a runnier paste forms.

- Place this paste into the sauté pan and heat gently. Add 200ml of water and combine, while bringing up to the boil. Once boiling, turn off the heat. Finally, add the coconut milk and Greek yoghurt to the curry paste in the sauté pan. Combine well. Leave to one side.
- By now your vegetables should be almost ready for the next stage. Once the 15-minute timer beeps, add the tomatoes and red pepper. Combine well and add a drizzle more oil if necessary. Return to the oven for another 15 minutes.
- Remove the vegetables from the halogen. Add these to your paste in the sauté pan. Add more water if you want a runnier curry, bearing in mind that some liquid will evaporate during the cooking. Cook for another 5–10 minutes until the vegetables are roasted to your taste.
- Sprinkle with coriander leaves. Serve with fluffy, fragrant rice, yoghurt and chutney.

75–150ml low fat coconut milk
1–2 tablespoons Greek yoghurt
2 tomatoes, cut into wedges
½ red pepper, deseeded and thickly sliced
Extra coriander leaves to garnish

Slow-Cook Tuscan-style Tomato and Beans

SERVES 2

1 small red onion,
cut into thick slices
3-4 tomatoes, cut into
thick wedges
½ red pepper,
deseeded and cut
into thick wedges
2 cloves of garlic,
roughly chopped
Olive oil
Balsamic vinegar
Sea salt
Sugar
Black pepper
1-2 sprigs of thyme
1 200g tin of
cannellini beans
75ml red wine

I love this dish. I tend to make a large batch and it lasts me a few meals – a lovely lunch with crusty bread, add pasta and you have a more filling meal, or simply on its own with a handful of crumbled feta. Delicious!

- In an ovenproof dish, add the onion, tomatoes, chopped pepper and garlic. Make the vegetables chunky but small enough to eat. Drizzle over some olive oil and a dash of balsamic vinegar. Finish with a sprinkle of sea salt, black pepper and a little sugar to help sweeten.
- Add the thyme sprigs and combine well, ensuring it is all well distributed and coated in the oil.
- Place on the medium rack and turn the temperature to 200°C. Cook for 20 minutes until the mixture starts to soften. You will be surprised how much liquid comes out of this.
- Remove from the oven. Stir in the cannellini beans and add the wine. Place back in the oven for another 10 minutes until thoroughly cooked and the beans are warmed through.
- Serve with crusty bread, add pasta to have a more filling meal, or simply on its own with a handful of crumbled feta.

Cauliflower and Broccoli Cheese Gratin

- Cut your cauliflower and broccoli into equal-sized florets. Steam or boil these until they are only just soft – they should still have a bite and a little hardness to them – you certainly don't want a soggy mash!
- Meanwhile place butter in a saucepan and melt gently on medium heat (not high!). Add flour or cornflour and stir well with a wooden spoon. Add a little milk at a time, continuing to stir to avoid lumps.
- Switch now to a balloon whisk. Continue to stir over a medium heat until sauce begins to thicken. The balloon whisk will also help eradicate any lumps that may have materialised. Add more milk as necessary to get desired thickness. It should be the thickness of custard.
- Add the 50g of grated Cheddar cheese, mustard and season with black pepper. Keep stirring until the cheese has melted. Taste to see if you need more cheese or seasoning.
- Place the cooked cauliflower and broccoli in your ovenproof dish. Pour over the cheese sauce.
- In a bowl, mix the breadcrumbs, oats, carrot and Cheddar cheese or parmesan together. Season to taste.
- Place this over the cauliflower cheese mixture.
- Place on the medium rack and cook at 200°C for 20 minutes until golden.

½ small head of cauliflower
½ small head of broccoli or bag combining both.
20g butter
15g plain flour or cornflour
200ml milk
50g mature Cheddar, grated
¼ teaspoon mustard
Seasoning to taste
60g wholemeal breadcrumbs
30g oats
1 medium carrot, grated
20g Cheddar or parmesan, grated

Note: You can often buy broccoli and cauliflower heads already bagged in the supermarket. It is more expensive than buying large heads but does avoid wastage.

150g plain flour
2 eggs
150ml milk
125–150g mature
  Cheddar, grated
½ small onion, finely
  chopped
6–8 sundried
  tomatoes (drained
  from oil), chopped
1–2 teaspoons fresh
  oregano
Seasoning to taste
2–3 tablespoons
  thick, good quality
  pasta sauce
1 tomato, thinly
  sliced

Eggy Pizza

This is a really yummy and very easy recipe. I saw Nigella making something similar and I wondered if it could be adapted to work in the halogen. Yes it can and it is a really big favourite of my youngest son. You can, of course, choose whatever topping and filling ingredients you wish, but I find this works wonderfully.

- Preheat the halogen oven using the preheat setting or set the temperature to 190°C.
- Place the flour into a mixing bowl. Beat the eggs and the milk together and pour onto the flour. Mix well. Add two-thirds of the grated cheese, along with the onion, sundried tomatoes and half the oregano. Season to taste.
- Pour this into a greased baking dish or tray – I use a Victoria sponge tin but you can use a Pyrex dish or anything with sides (making sure it fits in your halogen). Place on the high rack and cook for 20 minutes.
- Then spread the top of the omelette/pizza with your pasta sauce. Finish with the remaining cheese and oregano, and the slices of tomato. You could add anything else – pepperoni, goat's cheese instead of Cheddar, peppers, mushrooms, etc.
- Bake again for another 10 minutes before serving with a salad. A great supper!

Desserts

The dessert is really is my favourite part of a meal, and yes, my waistline will vouch for that! This chapter contains traditional family favourites – just because you are only cooking for 1 or 2, does not mean you should go without a delicious pudding! If you want to watch your calories, substitute cream with low fat crème fraîche or thick, Greek yoghurt.

Simple Bread and Butter Pudding

3–4 slices of white bread (ideally slightly stale)
Butter
30g sugar
30g dried fruit (raisins, sultanas or currants)
300ml full fat milk
1 egg
½ teaspoon vanilla extract

A delicious pudding that just screams comfort!

- Butter the slices of bread and place them in an ovenproof dish, layering with a sprinkle of sugar and dried fruit.
- Once you have built up your layers, mix the milk and egg together. Pour this over the bread and leave it to be absorbed for at least 20 minutes.
- When you are ready to cook, place on the medium rack and set the temperature to 190°C. Cook for 20–30 minutes until golden.

Note: I am a cinnamon addict so I always add a sprinkle of cinnamon between the layers.

Honey Roasted Plums with Almonds

It is not just vegetables that can be roasted – these plums are delicious when slow cooked – and they are perfect for the halogen.

- Preheat the halogen oven using the preheat setting or set the temperature to 180°C.
- Wash the plums. While they are still wet, roll them in sugar and place on a greased/buttered baking tray or ovenproof dish. Add 1–2 tablespoons of water or, if you are feeling a bit naughty, some liqueur. Place on the low rack and cook for 10 minutes.
- Drizzle over 1–2 tablespoons of runny honey and sprinkle with some cinnamon powder and almonds. Then cook again for another 10–15 minutes until the plums are cooked.
- Serve with custard, crème fraîche or ice-cream.

SERVES 2

4–6 plums, stones removed
Sugar
1–2 tablespoons liqueur, e.g. amaretto or Cointreau (optional)
Runny honey
Cinnamon powder
Sliced almonds

Lemon Saucy Pudding

25g butter
60g sugar
Juice and zest of 1
   large lemon
2 medium eggs,
   separated
1 teaspoon vanilla
   essence or paste
30g plain flour
150ml milk

- Beat the butter and sugar together until creamy.
- Add the lemon juice and zest, egg yolks and vanilla. Beat well before adding the flour and milk. This will form quite a runny batter. Give it a thorough stir to make sure there is nothing left around the side of the bowl.
- Meanwhile, in a clean bowl, beat the egg whites until they form soft peaks. Fold this into the batter gently.
- Line your baking dish with butter. I use a Pyrex baking dish but you could use individual ramekin dishes (see below). Pour in the mixture.
- Fill the bottom of your halogen oven with hot water up to approximately 3cm (1in). Place the baking tray in the water to create a *bain marie*. If you prefer and have room, you can place a baking tray filled with water on the lower rack and add small ramekin dishes filled with the mixture.
- Turn the halogen to 150°C and cook for 30–35 minutes (20–30 minutes for individual ramekin dishes). The pudding should have a golden sponge topping which is firm to the touch.
- When you serve the pudding, you will notice that the bottom half is a gooey lemon sauce and the top should be a lovely light sponge. Serve with crème fraîche or Greek yoghurt.

Baked Jam Sponge Pudding

These old-fashioned puddings are making a welcome comeback. Go on, enjoy!

- Beat the butter and sugar together until light and fluffy. Gradually add the egg.
- Sift the flour into the bowl and stir well, adding the milk and vanilla extract until a lovely batter is formed.
- Butter a 600ml (1 pint) ovenproof bowl or small ovenproof dish. Place the jam in the base before adding the sponge mixture.
- Preheat your halogen oven using the preheat setting or set the temperature to 180°C.
- Place the bowl on the low rack. Cook for 30 minutes until golden and firm to the touch. The sponge should be coming away slightly from the edges and should spring back when pressed. If in doubt, place a skewer or sharp knife into the centre of the pudding. If it comes out clean the pudding is done. If wet, place back in the oven and test again at 5 minute intervals.
- Serve with homemade custard.

SERVES 2

50g butter
50g sugar
1 large egg
50g self-raising flour
1 tablespoon milk
½ teaspoon vanilla extract
1–2 tablespoons raspberry jam

Gooey Chocolate Puddings

SERVES 2

175g dark chocolate
30g butter
75g sugar
2 eggs
1 teaspoon vanilla
  extract
1 teaspoon chocolate
  extract (optional)
30g plain flour, sifted
Icing sugar

These are baked in little ramekin dishes and turned out immediately – they will droop and ooze out chocolate when punctured with a spoon, but that is the general appeal. Serve with a dollop of crème fraîche and a few fresh raspberries for the perfect indulgent pud!

- Melt the chocolate using a *bain marie* or a bowl over a saucepan of hot water (don't let the bottom of the bowl touch the water). Once melted, leave to one side.
- Meanwhile, combine the butter and sugar until light and fluffy. Add the eggs, vanilla and chocolate extract. Combine well before folding in the sifted flour. Finally add the melted chocolate and combine well.
- Preheat the halogen oven using the preheat setting or set the temperature to 200°C.
- Thoroughly grease the ramekin dishes and then dust with flour. Pour in the mixture and place on the low rack. Cook for 12–15 minutes.
- Turn onto a serving plate, sprinkle with icing sugar and serve with a dollop of crème fraîche and some fresh raspberries – delicious!

Apricot and Pecan Crumble

This is delicious and so simple. Dried fruit is great to have in the store cupboard and in this recipe you can use all dried fruit, or you can add some tinned peaches.

- Place the apricots in a saucepan and pour over hot water until they are just covered. Leave to rest for 3–4 hours.
- When they are ready, add the orange zest and juice and the marmalade. If the water has evaporated, add a little more, enough to moisten the apricots and to give a sauce-type consistency to the fruit mixture.
- Bring to the boil and cook for 20 minutes, making sure the water does not evaporate (add more if needed). Place the fruit into an ovenproof dish.
- In a bowl, mix the butter into the flour until it forms a texture similar to breadcrumbs. Add the oats, sugar and pecan nuts and combine well. Place this over the apricots.
- Place on the medium rack and cook for 15–20 minutes at 190°C.
- Serve with a dollop of cream, ice-cream or crème fraîche.

75g dried apricots, halved
Zest and juice of 1 orange
1 tablespoon marmalade
1 tablespoon butter
40g plain flour
40g oats
30g brown sugar
25g pecan nuts

Rhubarb and Strawberry Crumble

500g rhubarb, cut
  into chunks
Handful of strawber-
  ries, whole or
  halved
30g sugar
30g butter
60g plain flour
30g oats
30g sugar

I love this combination. It is ideal for those strawberries that lack flavour or need using up, as they
transform into yumminess when you cook them.

- Place the rhubarb in a saucepan with a
  drizzle of water. Cook slowly on a medium
  heat until it starts to soften. You want the
  rhubarb soft but not completely mushy.
- Add the strawberries and stir in the sugar.
  Remove from the heat and pour into an
  ovenproof dish.
- Meanwhile, in a bowl, rub the butter into
  the flour until it resembles breadcrumbs.
  Add the oats and sugar. Cover the fruit with
  this crumble mixture and press down gently
  with the back of a spoon.
- Place on the medium rack and cook at
  200°C for 15–20 minutes.
- Serve with a dollop of cream, crème fraîche
  or ice-cream.

Rich Semolina Pudding

SERVES 2

350ml milk
30g semolina
30g caster sugar
Zest of ½ orange
1 egg yolk
30g sultanas
Nutmeg
Brown sugar

I adore these old-fashioned puddings. This is simple to make and gives a comforting hug on a winter's evening.

- Place the milk in a saucepan and heat until very hot. Then add the semolina and sugar, and bring to the boil, stirring constantly. The semolina will start to thicken. Don't allow it to stick or burn.
- Remove from the heat and add the orange zest, egg yolk and sultanas.
- Pour into an ovenproof dish. Sprinkle with a little nutmeg, brown sugar and extra orange zest. Place on the medium rack and cook at 180°C for 10–15 minutes.
- Serve immediately.

Marmalade and Apricot Bread and Butter Pudding

2–4 slices of white bread (ideally stale)
Butter
1–2 tablespoons marmalade
60g apricots
1 tablespoon brown sugar
2 eggs
30g caster sugar
300ml full fat milk
Zest of 1 orange

For chocolate addicts, add a handful of plain chocolate chips between each layer.

- Butter the bread on both sides, followed by the marmalade. Place the slices of bread into an ovenproof dish, so that they are slightly overlapping. While you are doing this, sprinkle chopped apricots and brown sugar between each slice.
- Mix the eggs, caster sugar, milk and orange zest together. Pour over the bread. Push the bread down into the mixture to ensure it is mostly covered. Leave to stand for 10 minutes.
- When ready to cook, place on the medium rack and set the temperature to 180°C. Cook for 30 minutes or until set.
- Serve immediately.

Raspberry Healthy Brûlée

SERVES 2–3

This is a really yummy dessert that takes just minutes to prepare. I tend to always have frozen raspberries in my freezer and yoghurt and crème fraîche in my fridge. This dessert looks and tastes far more impressive than it really is and the good news is that it is actually quite healthy!

- If you are using frozen raspberries, place them on your serving dish and put it on the high rack in the halogen oven. Turn to the Thaw setting for 10 minutes.
- Meanwhile, mix the yoghurt and crème fraîche together in a bowl. Once combined, add the vanilla paste and stir well.
- Remove the raspberries from the halogen. I tend to serve this in one serving dish but you could use individual serving dishes, though make sure they are heatproof. I keep the raspberries in the dish I thawed them in as it is heatproof. If you are using a different dish, or ramekin dishes, place the raspberries at the bottom.
- Spoon over the yoghurt mixture. Then sprinkle brown sugar – enough to form a generous layer to make the crème brûlée effect.
- Place back in the halogen oven on the high rack. Turn to the highest setting (usually 250°C) for 3–4 minutes, allowing the brown sugar to start melting and caramelising. The beauty of the halogen is that it enables you to see this cooking, therefore avoiding burning.
- Serve and enjoy!

100g frozen raspberries (or fresh)

150–200g Greek yoghurt (I use Total 0% fat)

2 tablespoons low fat crème fraîche

½ teaspoon vanilla paste

1–2 tablespoons brown sugar

Note: You can experiment by using blueberries or summer fruits instead of the raspberries.

Queen of Puddings

45g white bread,
  cubed
25g sugar
200ml milk
½ teaspoon vanilla
  extract or paste
25g butter
1 egg, separated
1–2 tablespoons jam
  (I use raspberry but
  feel free to use
  whatever you
  prefer)
25g caster sugar

My mum used to make this for us when we were children. Comforting puddings are making a well-earned revival; they are so much nicer than shop-bought, processed puddings.

- Grease an ovenproof dish.
- Place the cubed bread in a bowl and sprinkle with sugar.
- In a saucepan, heat the milk, vanilla extract and butter to almost boiling point and then pour over the bread and sugar mixture. Allow to cool. Then add the egg yolk and whisk until smooth. Pour this into the greased ovenproof dish.
- Preheat your halogen oven using the preheat setting or turn the temperature to 180°C. Place the dish on the low rack and cook for 30–35 minutes until set.
- While this is cooking, beat the egg white until it forms soft peaks, gradually adding half of the caster sugar.
- Melt the jam on a low heat as you don't want to burn it. Spread the jam over the set mixture. Top this with your whisked egg white. Sprinkle with the remaining caster sugar.
- Place back in the oven and cook for another 8–10 minutes until golden.

Apple, Chocolate and Hazelnut Crumble

SERVES 2

This is a seriously impressive crumble, especially when you soak the sultanas as this really does make the dessert. If you are adverse to using alcohol, you could opt for orange juice.

- Place the sultanas in a bowl and add the alcohol or juice. Leave them to soak while you continue with the rest of the recipe.
- In a large bowl, add the flour. Rub in the butter until it forms a texture similar to breadcrumbs. Add the oats, hazeluts, brown sugar and chocolate chips and combine well. Leave to one side.
- Place the apples in a heavy-based saucepan. Heat gently with approximately 1–2 tablespoons of water. Allow them to cook slowly until they are just starting to get soft but still hold their shape. You don't want it to be mushy or puréed. Stir in the granulated sugar and soaked sultanas including any leftover juice.
- Place the apple mixture in the base of an ovenproof dish. Cover with the crumble mixture and press down gently. If you want, you could add a sprinkle of brown sugar to the top of the crumble and finish with a sprinkle of hazelnuts.
- Place on the medium rack and set the temperature to 180°C. Cook the crumble for 20–25 minutes.
- Serve with custard, cream, ice-cream or crème fraîche.

40g sultanas
3 tablespoons masala, dark rum or orange juice
100g plain flour
50g butter
30g oats
40g hazelnuts, finely chopped
30g brown sugar
25g chocolate chips
2–3 cooking apples (depending on size), sliced or diced
1 tablespoon granulated sugar

Baked Apricot and Bananas with Dark Chocolate Sauce

2 bananas
3 fresh whole
   apricots, halved, or
   one small tin of
   apricot halves
Drizzle of runny
   honey
30–40g dark
   chocolate, melted
10g (1 dessertspoon)
   butter
15g (1 tablespoon)
   golden syrup

- Place the bananas, still in their skins, on one half of the baking tray. On the other half, add the apricot halves. Drizzle the apricots with honey.
- Place the baking tray on the medium rack of your halogen and cook at 190°C until the banana skin goes black and the apricots golden (this should take no more than 10 minutes). Remove the banana skins.
- Meanwhile, in a bowl placed over boiling water, melt the chocolate with the butter and the golden syrup. Then pour this over the baked bananas and apricots. Delicious!

Blackberry and Apple Upside-down Cake

SERVES 2

- In a saucepan, heat the 20g butter and golden syrup until melted together.
- In the base of your lined springform tin, place the sliced apples in a lovely fanned out pattern. I normally place the slices around the edges in a circle and then fill in the central gaps. Place some blackberries in any gaps.
- Pour the melted syrup mixture over the apple and blackberries. Leave to stand.
- Using your food mixer, beat the butter and 110g sugar until it becomes light and fluffy. Gradually add the eggs before folding in the sifted flour. Once mixed, add the vanilla and any remaining chunks of apple and blackberries. Cinnamon lovers could add a sprinkle of ground cinnamon.
- Carefully pour the mixture over the apple base. Gently level out the cake mixture without disturbing the apple layer below.
- Place this on the low rack and set the temperature to 180°C.
- Cook for 20–25 minutes or until the mixture is firm to the touch and an inserted cake skewer comes out clean.
- Remove the cake from the oven and leave for a few minutes, before turning out onto a heatproof dish. (Simply place the new dish on the top of the cake tin, face down, and flip over. The cake will then be bottom-side up on your new dish.) Sprinkle with icing sugar and serve hot or cold.

20g butter
20–30g golden syrup
1–2 Bramley cooking apples, peeled, sliced or chopped
Small handful of blackberries
110g butter
110g sugar
2 eggs
130g self-raising flour, sifted
½–1 teaspoon vanilla extract
Ground cinnamon
Icing sugar

Note: You will need to find a small cake tin – ideally about 15cm (6in) and springform.

Baked Banana Apples with Ricotta Cream

2 cooking apples, cored

1–2 soft bananas, mashed

¼ teaspoon nutmeg

½ teaspoon cinnamon

1 teaspoon lemon juice

1 tablespoons brown sugar

60g ricotta

30ml Greek yoghurt

½ teaspoon cinnamon

½ teaspoon vanilla extract

1 dessertspoon clear runny honey

I discovered this recipe in an 1970s good house-keeping book and thought it looked quite fun. I have adapted it slightly to suit tastes but it is perfect for the halogen. Serve with this delicious ricotta cream for some extra indulgence.

- Place the cored apples on a greased or lined baking tray.
- In a bowl, mix the banana, nutmeg, cinnamon, lemon juice and sugar together. Fill the cores of the apples with the banana mixture.
- Place the apples on the medium rack and set the temperature to 190°C.
- Cook for 30–40 minutes until the apples are tender.
- While the apples are cooking mix the ricotta and yoghurt with vanilla, honey and cinnamon.
- Remove the apples from the oven, place on your serving dish, with a generous dollop of the ricotta cream.

Cheat's Treacle Tart

If you love treacle tart, why not try this simple recipe. Using pre-baked pastry cases saves time and avoids soggy-bottom pastry! This recipe is perfect for the small pastry case found in super-markets (approx. 6–7 inch diameter)

180g golden syrup
15g (1 tablespoon) butter
25g double cream, (optional)
1 egg, beaten
50–75g breadcrumbs

- In a saucepan, gently heat the golden syrup until it becomes runny. Add the butter and stir well. Add the cream (if using), and the beaten egg and combine well.
- Add the breadcrumbs and stir well. You want a fluid consistency, not thick and lumpy, but with enough texture to give the golden syrup body.
- Pour this into your pastry case.
- Place on the medium rack and cook at 160°C for 30 minutes. If you need more time, turn the temperature down to 150°C and cook at 5-minute intervals, checking as you go to avoid burning. The pie should be firm and golden.
- Serve with a dollop of cream, crème fraîche or natural yoghurt.

Apple Pie

2-3 cooking apples, peeled, cored and chopped (Bramleys preferably)

1–2 dessertspoons of sugar, depending on taste

1 teaspoon ground cinnamon (optional)

1 handful of sultanas (optional)

¼ pack ready-made puff or sweet shortcrust pastry

1 egg, or a little milk to brush

Who doesn't like this family favourite? This recipe only uses a top for the pie as I find sometimes the bottom pastry can be a bit doughy – however, if you want to add a bottom, simply add a lining of pastry, baking it blind (bake with a layer of greaseproof paper and baking beans or pulses) for 10–15 minutes before adding the apple and the top. To ensure a non-soggy base you could brush the pastry bottom, once cooked, with egg-white or sprinkle with semolina.

- Peel, core and chop the cooking apples. Place them in a saucepan with 1–2 dessert-spoons of water. Sprinkle with the sugar, cinnamon and sultanas. Cook slowly so the apples just start to soften – you don't want them too soggy.
- Once ready, place the apples in the deep ovenproof dish. Roll out your pastry to the required thickness – I would opt for approx-imately 3mm.
- Brush the edge of the ovenproof dish with egg or milk. Carefully cut a strip off the edge of your rolled pastry, wide enough to cover the edge/lip of your ovenproof dish.
- Carefully place this over the edge of the dish. Push down to secure. Brush again with egg or milk.

- Using the edge of your rolling pin, roll up the edge of the pastry as this makes it easier to handle. Unroll onto the ovenproof dish. Push down at the edges to secure.
- Go around the edges of the pastry with your finger-tips making a crimping motion, making sure it is secure. Cut off excess pastry.
- Using a sharp knife, make two small slits in the top of the pastry to allow the air to escape. Brush with egg or milk and sprinkle with a little sugar.
- Place on the middle rack and set the temperature to 190°C. Cook for 20–25 minutes until the pastry is golden.
- Serve with custard or a dollop of cream or ice-cream.

Apple Nut Crunch

250g cooking apples, peeled, cored and sliced

1 tablespoon brown sugar

2 wedges of lemon

½ teaspoon cinnamon (optional)

40g honey-nut cornflakes (can use ordinary cornflakes if you prefer)

1 dessertspoon butter

I love simple puddings that don't require too much fiddling around but still give you a nice comforting dessert.

- Place the apple slices and the lemon wedges in your pan and cook until the apples are soft. You may want to add a little water to prevent them from drying out too much – about 2 dessertspoons should be plenty. If you want to save time on washing up, cook them in an ovenproof/hobproof shallow dish.
- Remove the lemon wedges and throw these away. Stir in the sugar and cinnamon and remove from heat.
- If you are not already using a shallow ovenproof dish, transfer the apples into one now.
- Cover the cooked apples with the honey-nut cornflakes. Dot the butter randomly among the cornflakes.
- Place on the medium rack and turn the heat to 240°C (you are effectively grilling the top). Cook for 5–8 minutes until golden.
- Serve immediately with a dollop of crème fraîche or natural yoghurt.

Baked Honey and Ginger Pears

SERVES 2

- Core, peel and halve your pears. Place them on a browning tray. Drizzle with a small amount of honey – try to keep this within the centre of the pears so it does not escape onto the tray as this may burn.
- Set the temperature to 220°C and bake for 10–15 minutes.
- While this is cooking you can crumble your ginger biscuits. Place them in a freezer bag and gently crush with a rolling pin.
- Remove the pears from the oven, drizzle with more honey and a sprinkle of mixed spice. Cover with the crumbled ginger biscuits.
- Place back in the oven and cook for another 5–10 minutes or until soft.
- Serve with a generous dollop of vanilla ice-cream

1–2 pears, cored, peeled, and halved
Runny honey
¼ teaspoon mixed spice
4 ginger biscuits, crumbled
Vanilla ice-cream

Simple Hot Chocolate Soufflés

Knob of softened
butter
2 teaspoons caster
sugar to line the
ramekins
50g dark chocolate
(at least 70% cocoa
is the best)
2 eggs, separated
25g caster sugar, plus
1 teaspoon extra
Cocoa powder or
icing sugar

Note: Serve with a
dollop of crème
fraîche for a
delicious, indulgent
pudding.

- Rub the knob of butter around the inside of the ramekins to help prevent sticking. Sprinkle 2 teaspoons of caster sugar over the butter to form a layer. Shake off any residue sugar.
- Melt the chocolate using a *bain marie* or a bowl over a pan of hot water, making sure the hot water does not touch the base of the bowl. Alternatively, you could melt the chocolate in a microwave.
- While the chocolate is melting, mix the egg yolks with 25g of caster sugar until they become light and fluffy. Add the melted chocolate and combine well.
- Whisk the egg whites until they form soft peaks. Add 1 teaspoon of sugar and whisk until thick.
- Add a spoonful of the whisked egg white to the chocolate. Once combined, fold in the remaining egg white.
- Preheat the halogen oven to 180°C.
- Spoon the mixture into the ramekin dishes. Level the tops off.
- Place on the medium rack and cook for 10 minutes, or until they are firm to the touch but slightly wobbly in the centre as you want them a bit gooey.
- Remove from the oven and sprinkle with cocoa powder or icing sugar. Serve immediately in the ramekin dishes with a side dollop of crème fraîche.

Index